The VIBES You FEEL

WHAT I'VE LEARNED ABOUT LIFE AND RELATIONSHIPS THROUGH THE HOLY SPIRIT

KIERRA SHEARD-KELLY

WITH VICTORIA MCAFEE

ZONDERVAN®

ZONDERVAN

The Vibes You Feel
Copyright © 2023 by Kierra Sheard-Kelly

Requests for information should be addressed to:
Zondervan, 3900 Sparks Dr. SE, Grand Rapids, Michigan 49546

Zondervan titles may be purchased in bulk for educational, business, fundraising, or sales promotional use. For information, please email SpecialMarkets@Zondervan.com.

ISBN 978-0-310-14162-4 (hardcover)
ISBN 978-0-310-14178-5 (audio)
ISBN 978-0-310-14177-8 (ebook)

Cover design: Cindy Davis
Interior design: Denise Froehlich

Printed in the United States of America

23 24 25 26 27 LBC 5 4 3 2 1

Contents

Introduction

Teach me to do your will, for you are my God!
Let your good Spirit lead me on level ground!

PSALM 143:10

Have you ever felt something deep down inside? Like a tugging or a pulling taking you in a different direction? Or maybe you've gotten a sensation that something isn't going right in your relationship, even though everyone around you says you make the perfect couple. A lot of times, those feelings are easy to ignore, especially when what the vibes are telling us is different from what we want to do. But the things we sense could actually be the Lord wanting to talk with us.

Because the God of the universe, the one who created us, wants to have conversations with the works of his hands.

Our thoughts are connected to the Spirt, who in turn connects to our mind. That's because there are intangible parts of ourselves intertwined and working together with God's Spirit.

The fact is, we communicate with God spiritually, with our

minds and our hearts. Since God is a spirit and we are a soul, there's a language—a connection—that is understood on a deeper and intangible level. As a result, it's up to each one of us to invest in that part of ourselves so we see the signals clearly and are able to interpret the messages God sends. And making sure we have a clear communication path both ways is key.

How do we create that clear path so we hear what God is sending?

How do we know the vibe we are feeling is the Holy Spirit—God's voice—and not just something we put together in our minds?

Thanks to social media, voices, sounds, advice, and challenges are coming at us 24/7. On top of all those other sounds crowding in, we also can be filled with shame, reminders of past accusations, and deep wounds that never fully healed. Or even a mindset we can't let go. I remember seeing a quote on social media I could relate to. I thought it was the Lord confirming what I was thinking. However, the Lord corrected me and said, "Nah, you're in your feelings." Trying to sift through the blur of everyday life—our internal voice, our thoughts, and the advice of well-meaning loved ones, friends, and others—makes interpreting the good, bad, and sometimes ugly comments a challenge and often frustrating. Hearing, and even dealing with the messages of the Holy Spirit God sends as our guide, can sometimes feel impossible or even overwhelming.

Especially as the human mind isn't capable of understanding everything about God and his mysteries, which includes exactly how the Holy Spirit operates in our lives. There are biblical concepts we won't comprehend until we see the Father face to face. But there *are* truths God has revealed to us that offer clear guidance, especially through his Word, which we can trust and rely on.

In the following pages, I'll unpack those Scriptures and the characteristics of the Holy Spirit as we explore who the Spirit is and how he operates in our lives. I'll also share ways we can better understand our inner vibes:

- Is this the Holy Spirit tugging me in a certain direction?
- Is this an unholy guide trying to pull me away from the Lord's guidance?
- Is this the Holy Spirit—or just me overthinking?

Throughout, we'll work to uncover the Holy Spirit's involvement in our lives, emotions, and insights, and tune ourselves to his voice so it becomes clearer and is the leading voice we hear. I've also created reflection questions in the back of the book for each chapter—and this introduction—which you can use to think more deeply about what God is personally showing you as you read.

I understand that writing a book about the Holy Spirit is risky. For centuries, people have disagreed about how God's Spirit manifests himself in our day-to-day lives. Some people believe the Spirit is quiet. Their places of worship are silent, and believers claim they have experienced the Holy Spirit's movement in a calm, still way, and they experience him silently moving in their lives. Then there are gatherings that are extremely vocal and loud, with shouts of praise to the Lord, a lot of movement, raising hands, and dancing. I grew up in this kind of church. And for a long time, I thought the Holy Spirit manifested himself by the speaking of tongues.

The older I get, the less judgmental I am of how God deals with individuals. I understand everything has to be measured by the Scriptures. For example, I don't see anywhere in the Bible where the Holy Spirit made anyone bark like a dog or disfigured someone's body. But I do see him speaking through a donkey or working through a gentle breeze. The Word of God highlights a variety of experiences.

My brother, J. Drew, is someone who has had many different experiences, and my adoration for him has helped me see others fairly and not judge so quickly. He's helped me grow to see that the Holy Spirit manifests himself in different ways, which has liberated me in so many covenantal relationships. My brother keeps a prayer life and has often been accurate with certain suggestions, warnings, and notes of love that he has shared with me along the way. For a long time, even as a kid, he's been an observer. I've noticed he watches and then chooses quietly. When I told him I was writing a book called *The Vibes You Feel*, he immediately agreed with the title and said, "That's exactly what it is!" He further explained, "It's the same thing, the Holy Spirit telling us something. We just call it vibes." I hadn't told him what the book was about at all other than the title, and still he knew what I was doing. So this was confirmation. I call him one of my personal prophets. We laugh about it, but he often confirms things in my life.

Moments like these are things I'd encourage you to pay attention to. Some of the moments we underestimate, or people we overlook, are actually defining experiences we should not ignore. For instance, someone may tell us something we need to know, but because we think we are closer to God than they are, we lessen the weight of their voices in our lives. Or have you ever noticed a vibe coming from your pet? How they respond to certain people? Since we are spiritual beings, instead of overthinking, we should consider and note when our innermost being picks up on something deeper.

For the moment, just rest in the fact that the Holy Spirit is God's power from heaven. He is always with us and around us. We can and do have access to the Holy Spirit's power. We can experience him in our lives—according to the Father's plans and purposes.

Please prayerfully read this book. And my prayer for you as you read is that when you come across something that hits you the wrong way or disagree with something I say, you won't toss the entire book aside. Keep reading. Ask the Holy Spirit to give you the insight and encouragement you may be needing to better discern the vibe within.

Chapter 1

The Unction: "Somethin' Told Me"

> But the Helper, the Holy Spirit, whom the Father will send in my name, he will teach you all things and bring to your remembrance all that I have said to you.
>
> **JOHN 14:26**

I went to the hospital for an emergency surgery. I asked God, "Why is it all happening to me?" Tears were in my eyes.

A friend of mine texted me right then and said, "Hey. Just checking on you. I keep thinking of you. Something told me to text and say a prayer for you. You good?" I cried harder because this was a moment the Lord was assuring me he hadn't forgotten me.

On another occasion, I was scheduled to attend a party. But everything under the sun seemed to happen that day and something told me not to go. Later, I found out some of my friends had gotten into an accident and some other issues also occurred that night.

These incidences—and a lot more like them—have made me think deeper about how the Holy Spirit works.

If you're like me, there have been many times when you've been sitting in an audience and the speaker said, "I didn't plan on saying this, but the Holy Spirit is impressing this on my heart and I've just gotta share it." Typically, a preacher or someone teaching the Bible may use the phrase "unction of the Holy Spirit." What they are expressing is a moment in their presentation when they are pressed to share something they had not anticipated sharing, often a sudden burst of understanding or insight into the subject or Scripture verse they were teaching. The feeling is so heavy or the thought repeated so often that it cannot be ignored or pushed away—it will not fade.

This same unction of the Holy Spirit can also happen to a Christian who is being prompted to do something (or not do something), say something, or go somewhere. It could be a strong urge to pray for something or someone in particular—right now! Countless stories are told about being woken up in the night because a loved one or friend came to mind. The next day, that prayed-for person shares about a near-death experience, an accident, or something that happened that very hour. Maybe we've called some of these experiences our "female intuition" or a "gut feeling," and have been casual about these moments as a result. However, we can't say God doesn't talk to us. He has proven that by giving us direction or conviction in many ways. Because God wants us to win, and really wants the best for us, he sends us guidance and answers. But it may seem as if he doesn't talk to us when we ignore his words.

Unction is also used in reference to times when something is being taught and the message becomes personal. People might say, "I felt like I was the only one in the room" or, "Pastor must have been reading my texts or listening in on my conversation." What they mean is the person speaking seems to know exactly what to say, even when they don't know what the listener is going through. That's because our Father knows the specific need, prayer request, or situation. He makes sure the person who has the need is in the audience.

This is a reason why a church family, or a pastor, is necessary. Sometimes certain people around us aren't as connected with the Lord as we may need them to be for a season, but if we are also surrounded by spiritually enriched, faith-filled communities, they may have the answers we need. These folks can help sharpen the unction, or confirm what we are feeling or hearing at times. The vibes must be right! The right vibe, and the right community, are essential for us to "become" and discover the mysteries we need to be aware of to thrive (see Colossians 1:26–27).

How can we be sure the "prompting" is from the Holy Spirit and not Satan, the flesh, or our own thoughts? These are the checks we need to run through our heads:

- The Holy Spirit will never, ever lead one of God's children to do something contrary to what's written in the Scriptures.
- The push from the Holy Spirit will always lead us toward Christ. He always points us in that direction, and it's

3

always toward seeking things that give us a deeper revelation of Jesus's identity.

- The Holy Spirit's message will always be one to build up, not tear down—moving us toward the good and opposing human impulses. This also refers to relationships. God's Spirit seeks to help his children to forgive and attempt to reconcile. The Bible tells us, "Be completely humble and gentle; be patient, bearing with one another in love. Make every effort to keep the unity of the Spirit through the bond of peace" (Ephesians 4:2–3 NIV).
- God's Spirit always gives a choice—follow him or don't. The Holy Spirit leads Christians. While he wants us to listen for our own good, he is not forcing us to do anything.

As a believer grows in their relationship with Christ, it will be easier to discern the voice of God over other voices. God's voice may not be audible, but inside we can have a sense of hearing, knowing, and understanding.

Be warned—Satan and the flesh are always at war within us, fighting against Spirit-filled promptings. The flesh interferes, Satan distracts and sometimes shows us how we can further our own agenda during these moments. The Word of God, godly counsel, and time in prayer are all ways our ears become sensitive to God's voice. As the song says, "Keep your mind stayed on Jesus." The writer of Hebrews reminds us as well, "Fix your eyes on Jesus" (see Hebrews 12:1–2).

Prayer

Father, I thank you for your Holy Spirit. Thank you for your patience with me, and for wanting me to have answers. God, I thank you for giving me a helper to assist me every day of this life you've called me to live. I ask that you forgive me for ignoring the details, the instructions, the warnings, your voice, or whatever else it is you've sent my way. Today, I acknowledge that the Holy Spirit is with me, and I am completely open to this relationship. I acknowledge your power. Thank you for being willing to project your Spirit to me to accomplish your will. You are alive in me. You are the force to be reckoned with. You are greater than any power. You gave your Son as my redeemer and your Spirit as my help (John 14:26). Thank you. I choose to listen. I thank you for giving this part of you, to intercede on my behalf (Romans 8:26). Forgive me for downplaying moments when you're speaking, as if it was something small. I choose to be better with you and will be more attentive to your nudges. Thank you for the unction from your Holy Spirit. In Jesus's name, amen.

Chapter 2

I Ran for My Life

*I wish that all were as I myself am. But
each has his own gift from God, one
of one kind and one of another.*

1 CORINTHIANS 7:7

I remember being about ten or eleven years old, sitting in a church revival as my mother got up to speak. I can still see myself in my brand-new brown and turquoise two-piece suit. It was my first time wearing a little heel on my black square-toe shoes. While the shoes didn't match this outfit, I made them work because they were my favorite! I felt grown up. But that outfit isn't what made this day so memorable.

As I listened to my mother preach a powerful message, God's Spirit fueled me and suddenly I was carried through the room. With my eyes wide open and filled with tears, I went running, ducking, and dodging people all around me like I had superpowers. "Holy Ghost, carry her! Run, run," I heard my mother calling out. I tried stopping, but my legs refused to obey. It was almost like they had a mind of their own. This is when I knew it was definitely the Holy Spirit! I cried even harder and agreed with the run. This was one of those "Holy Spirit encounters." In the past I'd laughed and teased people about dancing in the Spirit. Now, I was one who found it impossible to sit down.

In another service, while our home church was in revival, I felt the presence of God, but it was a different kind of experience. I cried out of desperation and repentance—overwhelmed, I wanted to show my seriousness—and felt so radical! I decided, *I'm going to do what I did last time.* However, the difference was I closed my eyes and started running on my own around the church. Next thing I knew, I'd tripped over a woman in the aisle and fell flat on my face. That day, as I lay there on the floor, I looked around and asked, "What happened?" It felt like I had tried activating the superpower, but it wouldn't work. I was highly embarrassed. However, I learned two lessons I have never forgotten. The first was, the power of the Spirit didn't happen by "me."

Don't fake.

Don't play.

Don't make the experience more than what God is asking for in that moment, and don't do something because everyone else is doing it. Only run, or move, when you know it's God.

The Holy Spirit is not an "it" for us to manipulate or control. It's not a "force" like in Star Wars. Nor is it some kind of fairy dust for us to grab in our hands from the air and fling around when we feel like it. We don't step into or out of this "thing." The Holy Spirit is God himself in our lives; his presence is with us.

However, even when we think we're being respectful, there are times we get ahead of ourselves and disconnect from the Lord because we let the human overtake the spiritual. I thought I could tell the Holy Spirit, "Come on, let's run again. That was fun!" The Lord made the truth about the Holy Spirit plain to me as I lay on the floor the second time I ran. He's not a play toy. And he is not under my control. When accepting this truth about my spiritual encounters, I then began praying the prayer, "Father, please never lift your hand from me. Please don't let me run without you because I don't want to trip and fall." This moment also reminded me I can't blame God for my mistakes, or think God allows bad things to happen to us. Sometimes, we try taking control but make things worse when it's his will to simply be still.

The second lesson God taught me was that his Spirit reveals himself in more than one way. As a child, he began to teach me reverence and how to acknowledge him with high regard. To move when he says "Go," and not on my own timing.

After my second run happened, I asked some family and friends, "Did you see me fall?" None of them had. I then felt like, *This was just a moment with God and me because it happened in the back of the church.* I've imagined I looked like Jacob wrestling with God. (Picture a human being wrestling in public with a spiritual being. That makes me laugh.) God was hiding me so no one would see my fall, and so what came after could be a conversation between him and me. This second spiritual encounter wasn't physical and showy, but that doesn't mean it wasn't *deep*.

During this time, I also sat in a Bible study and learned about the diversity of gifts. God lays out that truth in 1 Corinthians 12:4–10 (NKJV):

There are diversities of gifts, but the same Spirit. There are differences of ministries, but the same Lord. And there are diversities of activities, but it is the same God who works all in all. But the manifestation of the Spirit is given to each one for the profit of all: for to one is given the word of wisdom through the Spirit, to another the word of knowledge through the same Spirit, to another faith by the same Spirit, to another gifts of healings by the same Spirit, to another the working of miracles, to another prophecy, to another discerning of spirits, to another different kinds of tongues, to another the interpretation of tongues.

God is a master at giving his children a variety of spiritual gifts. Unfortunately, some of us make it about having a certain one. A few of my friends had been given the gift of tongues. I felt left out, as if my gift of singing and feeling the Spirit in my soul wasn't on the same level. I didn't feel unaccomplished. But when we react that way, it is like we're diminishing the Spirit and what God is specially preparing us to become through the gifts we have. Don't feel put down or lesser if he doesn't appear the way *you* expect him to or in a "big" way. There is no small gift with God if we're willing to fully accept what we have. From this Scripture in Corinthians, God tells us we can stand strong. He shows up for each of us in the way we need.

Additionally, as I studied, I found that I could relate with a few people in the Bible when it came to what happened to me when I danced in church that Sunday. The Israelites walked through the Red Sea on dry land, then watched their Egyptian enemies drown. Miriam, in her joy over God's protection, picked up her tambourine, then led the women in singing and dancing

(Exodus 15:20–21). The Bible even calls her a prophetess in those verses because God used her to speak to the Israelites. Another example is King David when he finally moved the ark of the Lord from the wilderness to Jerusalem. The king refused to contain his joy over bringing God back to his people. He danced before the ark as he moved it into the city (2 Samuel 6:14). And even when people tried to make fun of him—including one of his wives—David wouldn't stop because he knew his dancing pleased God, and that was all that mattered to him.

I got my turn, like Miriam and David, but I've learned the Holy Spirit never asks us do anything that would harm us or bring disaster. He always guides us toward experiences that bring us closer to God and serve the kingdom. He only wants the best.

Prayer

Father, I thank you for your grace. Forgive me when I move too fast or try to force what I think is right. And thank you for teaching me even in my most embarrassing moments. Help me stay connected with you—not for people's applause but for your smile. Help me to be spirit-driven and not self-driven. I see how fast and smooth I can go when I'm running with you, and also that when you're not with me, it can be a disaster. Holy Spirit, continue to teach and show me the difference. Have the necessary conversations with me while you shield me from ridicule. Amen.

Get Out!

> *I waited patiently for the LORD; he inclined to me and heard my cry. He drew me up from the pit of destruction, out of the miry bog, and set my feet upon a rock, making my steps secure.*
>
> **PSALM 40:1-2**

One of my first intense spiritual encounters happened while I was dating a certain guy. I was trying to get over my last boyfriend—a rebound situation. It also became a wake-up call when it came to my connection with God.

At this point in my life, I was often giving in to temptation while in a relationship. As a result, this new man and I went too far physically. But soon after, something began happening in me. My prayer life started to feel different. I remember wanting to practice self-discipline and to get right with the Lord. As I began reflecting and noticing the way I felt every time I gave in to my desires, it became clear I was choosing my flesh over my relationship with God, and those bodily desires began to diminish as I felt spiritual growth in the Lord. I also realized I wasn't happy in my relationship with this man. I refused to fall for just any old thing again.

So, one night, we began to argue when I refused to go further physically. He wasn't pleased with my answer, and we started arguing. In the darkness of the room, his anger began to appear to me. It was like a glow-in-the-dark experience, similar to what we see when playing laser tag. His spirit seemed to be like a green being.

The Lord enabled me to see the spirit driving this man. It stunned me. I began pleading the blood of Jesus internally. I repeated in my mind, "The blood of Jesus! The blood of Jesus!" At some point, I even whispered it.

I then approached this argument differently. I looked both him and the spirit driving him in the face and said, "Get out!" I meant it with everything in me. I didn't try arguing with the spirit I was feeling around me, or the spirit I was seeing.

I could tell he thought I was simply bowing out of the argument, but at this moment, it wasn't my place to try and prove anything. I was arguing with something deeper.

At that moment, I knew—*I'm fighting a different battle.* That was also when I realized it was time. Time for me to get serious about my walk with the Lord and time to get out of my old way of living.

Prior to this, the Lord had shown me things about my lifestyle and told me on several occasions, "Get out!" But I was a habitual dater—always in a relationship. Out of disobedience, I wouldn't let men go. But God had made it clear I needed to change my mindset, as well as remove myself from this relationship immediately. Otherwise, I was tying my soul not just to this man but also to the spirit driving him.

This incident happened years ago, but it always reminds me of Jordan Peele's movie *Get Out*. Chris, the main character in the film, became vulnerable after sitting for too long with his girlfriend's mother, who knew how to hypnotize him. As the mother found a way into his mind, he became a slave to her. And once he became privy to the fact she'd been hypnotizing him and so many others, he made up his mind to GET OUT!

When we aren't careful or obedient to the will of the Lord, we tie ourselves to people who know how to hypnotize us. Unknowingly, their influence can cause us to do things we had no intention of doing. When we aren't connected with the Lord, we can't discern, protect, or connect to the higher level of our calling.

On another occasion, someone I was seeing tried to use supernatural powers on me. Because I had become stronger in my mind and spirit by the time I was dating him, he had become more persistent and wouldn't leave. I was tired of his cheating. I kept mentioning I had grown out of love. I knew something wasn't right. My female intuition spoke clearly: it's time for you to get out! But for reasons I didn't understand at the time, I stayed.

One day, I found proof of what I'd sensed to be true. I knew this guy, and I KNEW he didn't live by the same spirit or with the same intentions concerning the Lord, but even then, what he'd been up to wasn't what I'd expected. I found out he subscribed to an online site that gave instructions on how to cast spells, and had been searching for spells that would help keep someone in love with him. When I came across this, I was completely shocked. I thought, *Now you're searching for* spells?" The Lord allowed me to see at face value what had been right in front of me. My nanna called it "stuck on stupid."

As I write of these two experiences, I am beyond grateful that the Lord delivered me. I am also glad that I wanted out!!! Tears fill my eyes as I write. The Lord saved me. He saw the agenda and intention behind every goal Satan tried to meet and went to war on my behalf. I am glad I wanted God enough to seek and chase after him, even while I was still a whole mess. Sometimes when we are in sin, we think we should give our relationship with God a break until we are ready to give him our all. Instead, I thought it was a good idea to stay with God as I got it right. I needed him to walk me through my mess.

Some call this hypocrisy. I call it practicing or exercising the faith. I wasn't, and am not, perfect, but I walked with the Lord and made things better.

No matter where you are in your walk with the Lord, you're never too far for him to reach out with signs of his presence. Those signs may be as small as a general sense of unease around someone or as big as a glowing green force in the darkness, but they are there if we only pay attention. Don't dismiss what your intuition is telling you—it could lead you away from a situation that might trap and harm you—and keep you from experiencing what God wants you to live.

I am grateful for the apprehension and hesitancy I experienced concerning these relationships and for any signals I experience now. I no longer question the things I sense, and I take them as memos from my heaven-sent messenger on the inside. The vibes, the instinct, the intuition, and the nudges are the Holy Spirit advising me to stay in or GET OUT!

Prayer

Father, I thank you for your guidance. Thank you for allowing me to know you are with me. Thank you for teaching me that what is important is something deeper than the flesh. The vibes I feel are often true. As I give more time to you, I am increasingly able to define the truth that you're revealing to me. It's a fight, but a spiritual one. I ask that you continue to help me. I understand this is a battle that I can give over to you. However, I do know it is my responsibility to refuel myself with your Word, ensuring I am equipped to complete my part of the work. Cleanse me from any unrighteousness. Today, I put on the full armor of you. Thank you for the helmet so that my mind is right in the fight. I put on the breastplate to guard my heart. I use the shield of faith to dodge any dart of darkness. In Jesus's name, amen.

Chapter 4

Eagles in the Sky

That the God of our Lord Jesus Christ, the Father of glory, may give you the Spirit of wisdom and of revelation in the knowledge of him, having the eyes of your hearts enlightened, that you may know what is the hope to which he has called you, what are the riches of his glorious inheritance in the saints.

EPHESIANS 1:17-18

There was a time in my life when I did a lot of road trips. On these trips, I kept seeing eagles. Cyndy, a woman who is like an aunt, traveled with me. She played a huge role in my life then and still does now, and I trusted her voice in my life because she too was a praying woman.

I told her, "I keep seeing eagles in the sky."

She said, "That's rare."

"Yeah! Like, are they even supposed to be flying around out here?"

She looked at me and said, "Maybe the Lord is using nature to speak to you."

"Oh," I said after a long pause. "He can do that?"

This challenged me to look into interpretations and do some research. I *carefully* searched on the internet, because social media can lead you to psychics, animal totems, and all kinds of craziness. This is where I remembered Mom's challenge to me about carefully, and prayerfully, seeking information while studying.

Once upon a time, I had been searching for answers on some spiritual questions I had and kept finding information that didn't match the right doctrine (1 Timothy 4:1). My mother was concerned about what I was taking away from the sources I found. She even hid some of them until the time was right, when I could better discern what was true. The truth of the matter is that I wasn't ready for some of the material I'd picked up. She challenged me and encouraged me to master the biblical basics (2 Timothy 2:15) and then pray about some of the information I'd read. This encouraged me because everything that is deemed spiritual in our world isn't always in alignment with Christian kingdom principles. This was my mother's way of guarding my spiritual gifts, guiding how I studied, and pushing me to learn how to sift false teaching from good teaching (2 John 1:10–11).

My parents have always been open to new revelation but stress there has to be Scripture to back it up. I remember bringing one crazy idea to a loved one and she said, "You done lost half of your mind!" As soon as she said this to me, I felt God behind her statement of correction, guiding me on how to search for the answers.

I share this experience because how you approach information has a spiritual component to it as well. When I first started my faith journey, I had a tendency to always seek answers in things my earthly self related to but not my spiritual self, so I remained desperate for answers as a result. But as I changed my mindset and tested what I read against the Word, I began seeing more answers from the Lord than I ever thought I would. I just needed to relax and trust him. And it was from that new mindset I carefully began searching by typing "scriptural references on eagles" and "what does the Bible say about eagles." Scriptures my family and I often quote immediately came up on my browser, but new Scriptures and commentaries came up that furthered my study:

"They who wait upon the LORD shall renew their strength; they shall mount up with wings like eagles" (Isaiah 40:31).

"Bless the LORD, O my soul, and forget not all his benefits, who forgives all your iniquity, who heals all your diseases, who redeems your life from the pit, who crowns you with steadfast love and mercy, who satisfies you with good so that your youth is renewed like the eagle's" (Psalm 103:2–5).

Interestingly, during the time I was researching eagles, I kept living in disobedience. But the Lord kept showing me eagles and speaking to me about them. God confirmed so many things in the Scriptures as I learned the science behind this bird. I didn't stop seeing eagles until I completed my study. Each day, the Lord revealed more to me.

Eagles build their nests higher than other birds. No other birds go that high to mess with their nest or their young. They also hardly ever come low to the ground. The parent eagles constantly care for their young from the moment the egg is laid, making sure they stay warm and are fed—even bringing them food after they leave the nest, while they're learning to live and hunt on their own. Eagles soar through the air, not flapping their wings, which helps them travel longer with less energy. The vision of an eagle is farther than the average bird's. While most humans have 20/20 vision, eagles are blessed with an astounding 20/5 vision. That means what looks sharp and clear to us at five feet is just as clear to an eagle from twenty feet away.

Job wrote about the characteristics of an eagle and the way it lives. They're not moved by people and their commands (Job 39:27). They find a secure home that keeps them safe, fixing their sharp eyes on their surroundings, staking out their prey from afar (vs. 28–29). And when the Bible wants to symbolize God's use of something strong and secure, eagle wings are often the reference used. John, while writing Revelation, spoke symbolically about eagles' wings. He pointed to them as shields that will protect God's people from the harm of the serpent (the devil) for three and a half years (Revelation 12:14).

The way eagles stay high above anything that could harm them and keep vigilant about their surroundings excited me, because a royal priesthood must do the same (1 Peter 2:9). And the fact that eagles use their powerful wings to conserve their strength and hunt more strategically than many birds made me reflect on how there's a way of living that is required of the believer that not everyone else will understand (1 Corinthians 2:14). Life may be hard for others who aren't walking with the Lord, but because we are often equated with eagles (Isaiah 40:30–31), we can mount up and soar, not having to flap our wings constantly to stay in the air. Life becomes easier when we allow the Holy Spirit to guide us. The strength he gives us is different. The vision he gives us is far greater. When I tap into what the Spirit reveals to me, I see and hear what the average eye can't see. This was the revelation for me as I matured in faith and saw the eagles in the sky.

God specifically used a gentle but strong note from Obadiah to remind me to stay humble. With all of the capabilities of an eagle, God is still in control. "'Though you soar as high as eagles, and build your nest among the stars, I will bring you plummeting down,' says the Lord" (Obadiah 1:4 TLB). I felt the conviction.

When you study God's Word, seek answers from the right place, and follow the nudges in your heart, you'll get what you need and be reminded of the lessons he shares. God speaks not only through your family and friends—he shares with you person- ally. The Word says he'll "reveal mysteries" to you. While studying the eagles, the Lord enlightened me. Pay attention to what you feel, in the Spirit, after you've gotten a revelation. Something as simple as an animal, billboard, or song on the radio can be a sign from God that you need to dig in and discover new things about yourself and your relationship with him.

What are some lessons you sense that feel like whispers in the mind, with peace and comfort to follow? How can you follow them today?

Prayer

Father, I thank you for allowing me to have encounters with you. As Job 12:7–10 tells us, you love me so much that you will call nature to show me a sign or get a message to me. You think that much of me. I understand I must be open to your greatness and not box you in with how I think you should, or will, speak to me. So open the eyes of my heart. Thank you for wanting to converse with me, and being willing to make this journey of conversation and relationship fun and interesting. While I am heeding your voice, I am also learning naturally and spiritually. I am excited to see the signs in the sky, and know nature bows at your command to simply get me an answer; tell me what's going on. Thank you, Lord. Keep talking. This'll be fun! In Jesus's name I pray, amen.

Chapter 5

Playing Church

> However, when He, the Spirit of truth, has
> come, He will guide you into all truth; for
> He will not speak on His own authority,
> but whatever He hears He will speak;
> and He will tell you things to come.
>
> **JOHN 16:13** NKJV

On Sundays when I was a kid, certain families would go over to Aunty Vickie's or come to our house after church, and I had friends I would play church with. I remember one particular Sunday, a bunch of us were in Aunty Vickie's living room, including my brother and a girl named Jessica. We played church and we played well, but at some point it turned into us crying out before the Lord in all seriousness. Imagine children between the ages of eight and twelve crying and worshiping the Lord with no adult help, on the living room floor.

The group of us had play instruments, a podium, and anything my brother J could find to use for the drums. I've never forgotten this—I remember it like it was yesterday. We sang our song selection and began going into the service as if we had a mini Day of Pentecost. What we had was special. No one teased anyone. It was all authentic. We were allowed to be who we really were in that space, and the Spirit responded.

This time of us worshiping wasn't the only time we played church and were met by the Holy Spirit. And over time, we learned sensitivity and respect through engaging in our own free worship and connecting with the Spirit. Those experiences are also how I knew the Holy Spirit's presence and leading wasn't limited to a particular age.

Of course, we had our parents guiding and teaching us when we were young, but we also believed what we were doing and experiencing was cool. We saw who God was in our parents' young adult lives. As we got older, some of my friends made their own decisions, of course, and I was in a crew later who thought the gospel was for older people to understand and that it didn't fully apply to them. But those of us who stayed close to the church clearly saw the blessings that could come when you stuck with God.

As I got older, though, those times of directly feeling God's presence weren't as frequent. I remember telling my mom I kept praying and praying and I felt like the Lord wasn't talking to me. She said to pray a "fleece prayer." She began to tell me stories of how she would pray. As an example, she would say, "Lord, if it's not your will, then don't let it happen," or, "Lord, if he's not your will, then move this person out of my life," or, "Lord, if it's not your will, then show me by not letting such and such happen."

Mom opened the Bible and gave me the example of Gideon. Then she made me do my research. So I went to the story of Gideon and learned he prayed the same kind of prayers. The Lord revealed himself and his answer the same way.

You can find Gideon in Judges 6. He was from a small tribe, but he became a military leader in Israel. God instructed him to rally the troops to fight the Midianites, who'd cruelly invaded the Israelites' territory. When God spoke to Gideon, the leader wanted to be sure he heard correctly. He asked God for a sign. Gideon put out a piece of wool overnight, asking God to make the wool wet and to keep the ground around it dry. In response, God put enough water in that wool to fill up a bowl. But Gideon still doubted. He asked for another sign, this time for the opposite to happen: the ground was to be wet but the wool was to stay dry. God did as Gideon asked. This time, Gideon felt assured Israel would be victorious over their enemy.

Some people knock Gideon, negatively comparing him to Joshua and Caleb, biblical characters who courageously answered God's call to go into Canaan without question. Personally, I'm thankful the Father did not leave out leaders who hesitated and had doubts. Moses went as far as to say to God, "Go find yourself another man" when God asked him to speak to Pharaoh; Peter denied knowing Jesus because he was scared of being killed. All of them—including Gideon—are heroes of faith. And to me, Gideon represents many of us. There are occasions when the Holy Spirit has to reveal himself several times and in several different ways. And it's okay. Gideon demonstrates God's loving patience with us.

I began praying my fleece prayers, literally asking for everything as a clear sign of some kind, and for God to answer if what I was asking was his will. However, I was sometimes in a mental space where, when things related to my prayers would occur, I would say, "Oh, that was just happenstance." So I began to downplay God's responses.

I started thinking my prayers were too impossible for God to achieve, or he wasn't talking to me in a clear way. During this time, my faith was in a different space due to my desperation. I really wanted an *exact* and obvious answer! I was praying things like, "Send shooting stars at my request." I know this may sound strange, but this is my truth. That was what I was doing to the Lord.

I had to correct my posture and spirit and my mind. I had to be willing to see the answers God was sending in his own way and the doors he was revealing to me. I couldn't consult with too many people about my experiences, as they would confuse me and make me discount what the Lord revealed to me. I also had to be careful to take my concerns to other believers who may have had just as big of an encounter.

While we can't control God or hold him to ultimatums, the Bible and human experience show that Gideon-like prayers can help us on our spiritual walk, giving us a way to see God's will when we need extra, almost concrete confirmation. Is there something in your life right now that you need a real answer for? Ask for a sign—but be open to the message God sends. It might be a spiritual encounter in your living room or the big shooting star outside your house, or it could be a video of a meteor shower that shows up in your TikTok feed as soon as you open the app. God moves mysteriously sometimes, but he always listens and communicates. He'll also place people in your life who can help you make sense of what he sends as part of his spiritual guidance and care.

Father, reveal more of who you are to me through your Spirit, Scripture, and conversations in prayer. I declare I'll live to know you and to have a true encounter with you. I ask that you come into my heart and help me see the joy in walking with you. You're fun to be with. Forgive me for sometimes treating you as if you're one-dimensional and can only operate one way, because you're multifaceted. You're a God of progression. My desires are your ideas placed in my heart. So forgive me for playing with you or feeling like you can't fulfill every need. What I've taken lightly, you've made serious, and I accept what's precious to you. Today I commit to growing in trust and understanding of who you are to me. I thank you for the conviction to not play church but to be the church, as that is the bride of Christ. I love you and I'm committed to you. Amen.

Who Is the Holy Spirit?

These things I have spoken to you while I am still with you. But the Helper, the Holy Spirit, whom the Father will send in my name, he will teach you all things and bring to your remembrance all that I have said to you.

JOHN 14:25-26

The person and work of the Holy Spirit is clear to us throughout Scripture. But because God is spirit (and the Holy Spirit is a connected-yet-separate part of God in the Trinity, which is its own mind-twister), we may not always understand *exactly* how the Spirit works in our lives because of our limited human understanding of spiritual things.

This is what we can know. The Holy Spirit possesses a mind,

emotions, and a will. He is leading, teaching, and convincing us from the time we are born, and especially works in our lives once we accept Jesus as our Savior. The Person of the Holy Spirit can be obeyed, ignored, grieved, blasphemed, insulted, or lied to by us because of our free will, but it will never lead us astray.

The Holy Spirit is not something just hanging around out there in the air.

He is present with Christians. In fact, the Holy Spirit has a personal home inside each one of us. As 1 Corinthians 6:19 tells us, "Do you not know that your body is the temple of the Holy Spirit within you, whom you have from God? You are not your own." And when we think about the temple as God's visible home in the Old Testament, this verse tells us God lives in each one of us as a sign that we are his temple, or church, on earth. This also means that, as part of a large church of believers connected through God's presence in us, our fellow Christians can help guide us through the leading of the same Spirit.

He knows all about us. "These are the things God has revealed to us by his Spirit. The Spirit searches all things, even the deep things of God. For who knows a person's thoughts except their own spirit within them? In the same way no one knows the thoughts of God except the Spirit of God. What we have received is not the spirit of the world, but the Spirit who is from God, so that we may understand what God has freely given us." (1 Corinthians 2:10–12 NIV). What this means is, because God is able to see and understand everything, through the Holy Spirit God is able to look deep inside us and uncover things that benefit us. And because he then passes along that knowledge to us through the same Spirit, we're able to understand and act on deeper things than people who don't follow God and listen to his voice.

Which leads us to the next amazing truth.

He has power to impart to us. On the day of Pentecost, God ushered in a new connection with his people. In the Old Testament, the Holy Spirit empowered designated people at certain times—like judges, priests, and especially prophets. But ever since Pentecost, all believers are filled with God's Spirit.

Acts 1:8 tells us, "But you will receive power when the Holy Spirit has come upon you, and you will be my witnesses in Jerusalem and in all Judea and Samaria, and to the end of the earth." So as believers, not only can we reach out to other people and share what the Spirit tells us, we are given power that helps us spread the gospel as well—which sometimes means being given extra courage, special opportunities, or other amazing gifts when needed.

And in Joel 2:28–29, we're told about this post-Pentecost time, "And it shall come to pass afterward, that I will pour out my Spirit on all flesh; your sons and your daughters shall prophesy, your old men shall dream dreams, and your young men shall see visions. Even on the male and female servants in those days I will pour out my Spirit."

He has been in existence since the beginning of time. As part of the Trinity, the Spirit took part in creating this world. As Genesis 1:2 tells us, "The earth was formless and void, and darkness was over the surface of the deep, and the Spirit of God was moving over the surface of the waters" (NASB). And he continues to be active in maintaining and sustaining it.

He speaks. God gives instructions to people in our world through the voice, influence, and nudging of the Holy Spirit. One clear example of this is in Acts. "The Holy Spirit said to Philip, 'Go over and walk along beside the carriage'" (Acts 8:29

NLT). Because of this nudging, Philip was able to talk with someone who was seeking to learn more about Scripture, and then baptized him. In this case, the Spirit swept Philip to a location where he was needed.

He makes decisions. The New Testament church depended on the Holy Spirit for exact details of what to do, where to go, and how to arrange things. Again, Acts (a book that talks a lot about the Spirit) gives us a view into how the early Christians learned to listen to the Spirit's guidance. For example, in Acts 9:17, the Spirit helped the apostles accept Paul into the church. If they'd listened to their heads, they might have never accepted their former persecutor, who after being received went on to become one of the greatest spreaders of the gospel. The church leaders also relied on the Holy Spirit's guidance when it came to missionary journeys—who to send and where—as well as for other key decisions they needed to make. To prepare themselves for guidance, believers then did a lot of the same things we can do now—pray and fast—or stay away—from things that could distract us from God's message.

He can be grieved. The Holy Spirit can experience deep emotional pain and sadness. Especially when God's children block his work in the world, take sin lightly and/or carelessly, when the door is opened to Satan, and when worldly things are cherished. Because again, above all, the Spirit and God want what is best for us, always.

Chapter 6

Mind-Body-Vibe

> *Come to me, all who labor and are*
> *heavy laden, and I will give you rest.*
> **MATTHEW 11:28**

We've been talking a lot about the Spirit's guidance and presence in our lives, but another big part of our spiritual life—and the Spirit's part in it—has to do with how God created us to be and function physically and mentally.

God created us as body, mind, and soul. The problem is, some people in our modern society break those things into three separate categories and think like Gnostics, an ancient group from back in Bible times. This group emphasized and taught that the physical body is evil and all that matters is the spiritual. This is not true. Jesus pointed to our various parts and how they are connected when he said, "And you shall love the Lord your God with all your heart and with all your soul and with all your mind and with all your strength" (Mark 12:30). It's pretty hard to do all those things if some parts don't matter!

Jesus also took several opportunities to rest his body and mind, seeing both as important to his overall spiritual health. During those times, he got away by himself for solitude and to commune with the Father. And while anything from Jesus's mouth is pretty hard to argue with, for even more proof Paul said to offer one's whole body as a living sacrifice to the Lord, not just your souls or the spiritual part of yourself (see Romans 12:1–2). That's because what we do with—and for—our bodies helps us build and strengthen our faith.

An excellent example of how our body, mind, and emotions are connected is the chemical in our bodies called dopamine. (Bear with me, because we're about to get scientific.) This chemical is released from our brain and into our body to cause pleasure, satisfaction, and motivation. It is the reason people enjoy food, physical relationships, an accomplishment, receiving financial gain, or winning. However, when dopamine is released into our bodies it also triggers our minds. This has to do with the flesh of our being—the science of our makeup. The dopamine reinforces our behaviors, because when something feels good, we want to do that thing again and again.

Soon, things that are fine in moderation—like food—become problems, and things that often fall outside healthy behaviors— like alcohol, gambling, drugs—can take over our lives. As an example, when we partake in pleasures that aren't beneficial, it can cause a struggle inside of us because the physical part of us doesn't want to stop, and we find our spiritual part falling out of God's will as our desire to do what he calls us to do fades. And that struggle must be recognized. Take it from me; I've been there at times. If we don't do things God's way, it is not good for our spirit.

Too much *or* too little dopamine is also a problem. Low dopamine levels can cause a decrease in motivation, mental illness, or depression. On the other hand, too much dopamine may cause a person to be too competitive, aggressive, go off on binges, or become deeply addicted.

That means just the right amount of dopamine is essential for your body and brain. The chemical serves as a messenger to your nerve cells. This one element inside us can affect our memory, body movement, concentration, learning, and sleep for bad or for good. And the things you can do to boost your dopamine are also things that match up with things God made to be beneficial, like addressing emotional or mental problems, eating less sugar and more healthy foods, or getting more sleep. This includes exercising, periods of stillness and quiet, or getting a massage. Thinking positively, being thankful for things in your life, and laughing rather than criticizing and complaining also help to increase dopamine levels.

Another way to increase dopamine levels is self-care. This practice is important for your mind, body, and spirit. You move differently when you reward yourself and intentionally send these signals scientifically and spiritually. You make choices that will help to continue the rewarding ways of life. What does self-care look like to you? Make a list. (Maybe it's sleep, relaxing, vacation, a long drive, reading the Bible, time with a good friend. Even what we call "retail therapy." Managing our funds well and achieving a financial goal can also be rewarding—so responsible retail therapy!) What did you write down? When was the last time you did any of those things? Maybe it's time to treat yourself.

At this point, part of you may be arguing about this topic of self-care. Especially if it goes against things you might have been told while growing up.

Is self-care biblical?

Shouldn't we as Christians be churchin' 24/7—no breaks?

Won't God take care of our minds, bodies, emotions, and all the rest even when we overdo it?

No way I can do self-care. I have my school, a job, networking for my future, and a lot of stuff tugging at me.

Throughout the Scriptures, we see the Father pointing his children toward times of rest and refreshment. But nowhere is there a passage pushing us to continuous work.

God never grows weary or tired, but we are not God. We, as human beings, have limits. After a powerful ministry time, God pulled Elijah away to rest (1 Kings 19). He fed him, let him sleep, and then gave him new instructions on how to move forward.

"I'm just burning out for Jesus" has become popular among Christians. Sounds good, but it's not biblical. In our money-hungry society, individuals often have too many balls in the air, trying to survive financially. Any compassionate person in ministry knows it is easy to get overburdened with people's problems and issues. Just day-to-day responsibilities can be overwhelming at times and lead to burnout.

Jesus knew our tendency to overwork ourselves, so he talked about rest. "Come to me, all you who are weary and burdened, and I will give you rest. Take my yoke upon you and learn from me, for I am gentle and humble in heart, and you will find rest for your souls. For my yoke is easy and my burden is light" (Matthew 11:28–30 niv).

Burnout can also result from being too dependent on yourself and not leaning enough on the Father. You may need the Holy Spirit to examine your heart (and your workload). A task may need to be delegated. For example, Moses's father-in-law helped him when Moses had taken on too much while leading the Israelites (Exodus 18:14–23). Another example comes from the apostles. They realized they were carrying too much in the early church and decided to delegate responsibilities to other leaders (Acts 6:1–6).

We also need to be careful we don't find ourselves playing the martyr. People-pleasing can be exhausting. Is there a need to say, "No, I just can't do it this time"? Under the Holy Spirit's guidance, we can stay balanced. God sees us as valuable. He's not out to wear us out, so lean on the Spirit.

The main concept behind the mind-body-spirit connection is that we are all more than just our thoughts. We are also our bodies, our emotions, and our spirituality. All these things combine to give us identity, determine our health, and make us who we are.

Your body responds to your thoughts and emotions, which results in your actions. What you experience and feel inside is not just a vibe. Your thoughts and feelings affect your health: mentally, spiritually, and physically.

Prayer

Father, I thank you for wanting me to feel fulfilled here on earth. Though my soul longs to be with you, you have made sure I experience you here on earth. I ask that you allow me to be aware of my needs. Show me how to meet those needs through prayer, conversation, and rest. Anoint me to have the balance necessary to succeed in your eyes and serve your people. Strengthen my body. Remove sickness. And if there is sickness, make that a part of my testimony; refocus me to know your will. Build me up so that in everything, you get the glory. Thank you for your grace. Fill me up. Allow my spirit to connect with you freely. Remove any weights of bitterness, unforgiveness, shame, worry, anxiety, depression, or guilt. I promise to listen when my body is saying I need a break. I will acknowledge my emotions but admit that I am the master of how I feel and process. I will give you time to ensure that my spirit is enriched and filled with Scriptures. Solidarity is my portion. Rest is my portion. Thank you for the quiet places you've given me to restore and retreat. Amen.

Chapter 7

Knocked Off Your Square

> *Be sober-minded; be watchful. Your adversary the devil prowls around like a roaring lion, seeking someone to devour.*
>
> **1 PETER 5:8**

One of my favorite movies is Marvel's *Black Panther*. I often think of the scene at the start when T'Challa fights M'Baku. T'Challa is losing the fight for his kingdom when his mom yells out, "Show them who you are!" I get chills as the fight takes a turn and T'Challa begins to win the fight, to the point of him having to show mercy on M'Baku. This is the same thing the Holy Spirit does with us. His vibe always wants to remind us of our identity and show the world who we are in Christ.

At certain times in life I've thought, *My life isn't clean enough to access parts of the kingdom.* I didn't feel like I had power and authority. In those moments Satan tried to knock me down and keep me off my square. He does anything and everything to knock us down. He wants to make us feel like we should think twice about what we are called here to do. He wants us to question, "Is this the Holy Spirit speaking or just me hearing things?" He wants us to stay in a state of confusion and doubt.

But God is not a God of disorder; he's a God of peace (1 Corinthians 14:33). Satan wants us to feel like our vibes are in error, that we can't rely on our intuition and experiences. God, however, is right there, on point, whenever we feel an inkling of concern about the spaces we are in, the people we are seeing, or the plans we are making—and uses those moments to give us confidence in who and whose we are.

I've seen what trusting God's vibes can do. When I was younger, I often got nervous about going out to sing. I knew my calling wasn't just entertainment but blessing people with what I did on (and off) stage, but the urge to stay off the stage sometimes had me doubting that call. Once I began really living like Christ—trusting the Lord and walking in new confidence from understanding the authority I was given as a King's Kid—I understood the Holy Spirit is always with me, empowering me and leading me where I need to be. This way of thinking and living doesn't come overnight, but with practice it becomes a lifestyle—an obtainable way of life. It takes some sacrifice, but life is much better when living on this higher level. And while I am still not perfect, now there are some vibes, challenges, and spirits that know not to play with me.

The truth is, we deal with some things we are called to dominate, and we often settle for less because we aren't clear where we stand with the Father. Or we listen to the voices of the world—the devil—instead. If you look at 1 John 4:4–6, this reality is clear: "You, dear children, are from God and have overcome them [evil spirits], because the one who is in you is greater than the one who is in the world. They are from the world and therefore speak from the viewpoint of the world, and the world listens to them. We are from God, and whoever knows God listens to us; but whoever is not from God does not listen to us. This is how we recognize the Spirit of truth and the spirit of falsehood" (NIV). As you read this, I hope you know God is with you wherever you go. We are called to be overcomers, called to win!

One of the greatest stories in the Bible that's challenged me is when demons talked to Jewish leaders who were trying to drive out the evil spirits. The demons implied they weren't coming out of the man because they didn't know who was trying to cast them out. The demonic spirit spoke back, "Jesus I know, and Paul I recognize, but who are you?" (Acts 19:15). The Jewish leaders ended up running out of the house naked after the demons attacked and overpowered them. As a young person, this story scared me. But as I grew older, I understood that all it took to stand up to evil was to be authorized. My father always challenged me, "It's not for me to have conversations with demons, but to simply cast them out." The Jewish leaders in the book of Acts had no idea how to activate the power of the Holy Spirit. They lacked insight and knowledge about how to fight this fight.

Is this story in the Bible—and others like it—placed there to scare us? Not at all. They're to show us that some things are deeper than we see. The enemy is clever and desires to sift us as wheat (Luke 22:31). Hence, dominate! Don't let Satan dominate or make you feel inferior. God is with you. The Holy Spirit is nudging you, informing you—show them who you are!

Satan uses people as distractions. Sometimes in passing, someone will say something to us, and depending on where we are within
ourselves, we may never forget it. We may live with it as a lesson
and look to improve, though more often it may lead us to feel inad-
equacy or doubt. But what was the real vibe behind the statement?
This is more reason to pay attention to the initial vibes we feel,
because this insight helps us navigate differently. It informs us of
what to listen to and what not to listen to. The Holy Spirit wants us
to live life with answers. At the end of the day, we make a choice.
Paying attention to the spirit or vibe behind what we encounter will
let you know if it was from heaven or hell, or if it came from good
intent or malice. The more practicing and sensing we do, the clearer
we are on whether it's the Holy Spirit or the world.

Let's think about this a little deeper. Ever walked into a room
and just felt weird? There's a spirit behind it all, and it could be
from the light or the darkness. Determining which means testing
that vibe against what the Bible tells us about God, and often
asking for clarity. (Because again, our God has us when we need
him and sends signals for our good.)

Or maybe you've been in a friendship or other relationship
that makes you question whether it's good for you or not. For me,
I've often spoken with someone and gotten exhausted after chatting with them. Spiritually, they drained me. I wanted to step away,
but as I took time to think about my interactions, it was clear I
was being called to help them—in a way that left me still feeling
spiritually full. Maybe you've had a similar experience. They can
happen because sometimes we are so connected with the Lord,
others unintentionally pull what they need from us because their
soul needs it. Those people may be experiencing so much hell on
earth that their spirit gravitates toward the closest thing to heaven

they can find. In this and other things, the Lord dealt with me about the things I once ignored. He had me understand the wisdom and insight he shares with his children through his Spirit.

Every bad vibe you feel isn't a call to escape—it may be a call to pray for help. I've had to seek the Lord for more direction so that I wasn't giving more than I was supposed to, overlooking things I needed to pay attention to, or committing myself to the wrong assignment. But every vibe is a chance to show the world who you are and want to be.

Father, I thank you for wanting me to win and letting me represent you. Thank you for making me strong in the faith. You've given me skills, gifts, and talents that help me navigate the world and make a difference. You've also given me authority as your child. Today, I acknowledge I am much better with you as my guide. I crucify the flesh today and ask that you continue to show me you and your plan so I am following your call. Let your Holy Spirit constantly remind me of who I am in you. Sometimes, the vibes of defeat are the enemy's way of getting us off our square to operate on a lower wave. Sometimes the vibes we feel are of condemnation, which isn't of Christ. So, I choose to show them who I am in you, and let there be no shame in your game. Please give me the strength to walk upright and not fall into the devil's trap. I need you constantly cheering me on, so I feel your push in the Spirit. Amen.

Chapter 8

Checkmate or Check Yourself

> *When the Spirit of truth comes, he will guide you into all the truth, for he will not speak on his authority, but whatever he hears he will speak, and he will declare to you the things that are to come.*
>
> **JOHN 16:13**

My husband, Jordan, and I agreed we wanted to wait a year to get pregnant. So many people kept asking, "When are the babies coming?" Or they would say things like, "Y'all not doin' enough!" in a joking manner. Soon I got distracted, and I began rushing things.

Jordan stayed the course and stood firm on our original agreement. He isn't easily moved by others' suggestions. One of the most attractive things about him is how unimpressionable he is.

He makes a decision and sticks to it, especially when it's approved by the Lord. He's the epitome of "I have set my face like a flint" (Isaiah 50:7). A flint rock is a hard, unmovable stone. The Bible references that use the word usually describe a person with firm determination.

Jordan and I enjoyed our first year of marriage. My husband and I agreed and intentionally used the time to get to know one another and teach each other as a married couple—before we brought children into the picture. We wanted to use that time for ourselves. But there were times during that year I forgot Jordan and I had already agreed with the Holy Spirit. I allowed other people's questions and opinions to rush me. I was irresponsible with my emotions. As a result, I mentally stepped out of my agreement with my husband and the Lord. I started asking, "What's wrong with my body? Why am I not getting pregnant?"

Jordan finally said, "We had always said a year. That was the time God approved. His timing is everything."

A checkmate moment. Jordan's comments confirmed I was out of bounds, off from God's timing. Not only out of God's timing, but now moving outside of what the Lord had told us. I started concentrating on what others thought. As a result, while having fun and living life with my husband, I began moving at my own pace.

Sometimes the Lord speaks in casual conversations, but it's up to us to always prioritize and value his instruction. When I started to get back on track, I evaluated myself and noticed I have a tendency to move when I feel pressure. I often forget the plans I discussed with the Father and feel behind because of external sources.

But during the times I felt pressure, I even began comparing my life to others, which again is out of bounds (Galatians 6:4). I became fearful because of the stories I had heard about women not being able to get pregnant. One of our counselors told us, "Their horror story does not have to be your horror story." That's when I checked myself and began moving with the Lord and trusting his timing. My feelings and not the Spirit had completely moved me, when it should have been the other way around.

What are you getting from the vibes within yourself? Sometimes our intellect can detach us from what we feel. Sometimes what we feel during, or from, a moment has nothing to do with God's Spirit. That's the part I had to come to grips with. It's easy to be distracted and agree with the negative feelings or others' suggestions.

Maybe you're in the same boat when it comes to God's timing: you rushing yourself, others rushing you, or always questioning what you think is best. It could be schooling, college prep, or a new job. Remember to hear what the Lord is saying about the next steps. Think: *Is this me feeling pressured? Or a decision I feel really good about?*

Many times, I go back and forth about something because I'm in my feelings. Being in your feelings can get very heavy very quickly. We become wrapped up in only what we want to see. We don't assess correctly and this can cause us to make unreasonable, hasty decisions.

An example of being in my feelings was when an advisor once told me I needed to be delivered from people. Deliverance has to do with being free from bondage. For example, the Hebrew children in Egypt lived in bondage. Their slave masters controlled everything—where they lived, slept, daily activities, meals, and how many children they had. So God sent Moses to deliver his people and set them free. In the same way, I'd gotten caught up in allowing others to influence my plans and voice and control how I acted. I couldn't hear the Holy Spirit. I needed to find the balance of embracing good counsel versus unhealthy pressure so I could be set free. I didn't want to be rebellious because I believed that some of these influences were there to help me, but I needed to not worry so much about people's opinions.

At the time, my advisor's comment about my need to be delivered from people didn't rub me right. I wasn't mature enough to understand. So, I dealt with her from an attitudinal place until one day, in my late twenties, it hit me she had been telling me the truth all along. I called and apologized to her. I was so in my feelings that I couldn't receive the truth. If I had accepted what she said, I would have been set free so long ago. And our relationship—and my relationships with other people—wouldn't have suffered. I had distanced myself from her because I was in my feelings. I began living my life to avoid those kinds of conversations with her and others. I responded to things from this mindset. I was always "ready" because of how I continued to approach this area of my life. I would deal with people from the place of my feelings being hurt and did not operate at face value. In this case, this was about what my body was feeling more than my spirit.

For a long time, almost every person who encountered this "hurting Kierra" got the wrong vibe from me. Once I accepted this truth—that if I am easily swayed by worldly things rather than by the Spirit, I'll always have a problem (James 1:8). I had to allow myself to be delivered from people and remember from which place I operate. I had to work on not being easily offended. I had to be open to healthy relationships and learn to manage good connections.

And those healthy relationships are the key to checking

ourselves. Think about the people in your life who have a close relationship with God, or who aren't easily swayed by someone's comments. Ask them for guidance if you can. Or talk with someone in your church whose opinion you trust when you sense yourself spinning away from what you and the Spirit have landed on. We don't have to lead ourselves into a checkmate situation, because God gives us the tools and teachers to help us make the right moves.

Father, I thank you that everyone else's story is not my story. I thank you for your Holy Spirit, who convicts me by telling me when I am out of bounds. I ask that you continue to help me operate in the territory you've authorized. Help me operate in the land you have called me to. Help me operate in the time you have approved. Father, I ask that you forgive me for not trusting your Word. Father, forgive me for going outside our conversations and then trying to do the opposite of what we've agreed. I ask that you allow your Holy Spirit to continue living inside me as a welcomed presence. I'm grateful your Holy Spirit has me examine myself. Father, help me know the difference between a healthy examination and over-criticizing myself. As long as I am out of my feelings and driven by your Spirit, I can be at peace while sifting, filtering out the toxins or damage that may prohibit me from being all you've called me to be in purpose and in relationships. Amen.

Chapter 9

Conversations vs. Prayers

Let your speech always be gracious,
seasoned with salt, so that you may know
how you ought to answer each person.

COLOSSIANS 4:6

I've learned when there is a vibe, or you hear something from the Spirit while you're around someone close to you, a conversation may be in order. The question we have to ask, however, is whether that conversation is mainly with God or if we need to directly speak with the person.

To be clear, we can always go to God to talk through what we're dealing with—he's there to help us make sense of any experience. We can go to him in prayer at the start of the situation, while we're dealing with the person, or at the end to get clarity on what happened. But we *really* need to go to God first when we sense a conversation with the person will not solve a core problem—because it's about what is going on in your heart. When you sense a situation developing, take a moment to reflect: Does the vibe you feel make you think more about something in yourself than about something you have to address with the other person? Or does the vibe tell you that you need to stay away from that person for a while for your mental and spiritual health? Addressing things with the other person before we address them through prayer and receive guidance might end up hurting us or the relationship.

Ultimately, the truth is, some things need to be directly resolved through a conversation with the person who gave us the vibe. Can conversations steal your joy? Of course. Can they help you come to a resolution? Absolutely. Conversations can do both. But any discomfort or pain are often worth it. For example, sometimes the vibes we get are because our friend or relative needs the conversation—we're being called to share wisdom or remind them of a truth they need to face—and sometimes this vibe is a signal that we need to engage in or work through the relationship for a future good on both sides. Even if that future seems impossible and not worth the current hassles.

I had a tendency to walk away from people when it became too much. A family member I trust challenged me to begin having more conversations to resolve matters rather than cutting folks off too quickly. He challenged me to extend grace. This was a great challenge for me. I've grown in this space, especially as I began learning how to "live accordingly." That includes making a mental note to check my approach, and not being frustrated when I don't receive the results I am looking for. The truth is, everyone has a right to make their own decisions and do as they see fit.

There are some things we simply cannot change and are called to accept. Not everyone shares the same dreams and desires. We all have different motivations and ways of approaching life. As close as we may be to someone, we still may not be in the same place in the Spirit all the time.

But even with the idea of grace, the impulse to end a relationship can still be strong. One of the most disheartening things is having to consider if, after having longevity in relationships, things need to change. Different paths can still occur even after being good with someone for many years, and those paths can lead to confusion. *Breakup* isn't just a word we use with someone we've been dating; the same kind of urge to split up can happen in our platonic relationships or sisterhoods. At one point in my life, I found it harder to break away from guys who were very toxic in a dating relationship than ending things with a homegirl/friend I just needed to forgive (or ask her to forgive me).

This was when I started learning perseverance and sacrifice. Being committed doesn't mean allowing nonsense, even though I thought that's what it was about for some time. It also doesn't mean there's a checklist that needs to be followed to keep the relationship solid. My family member and I talked more and more about it. When I went home, I researched to see if I was rightly interpreting the Word and living how I should. I found we are most definitely supposed to show grace and forgive our neighbor, however many times it takes.

> Then Peter came to him and asked, "Sir, how often should I forgive a brother who sins against me? Seven times?"
>
> "No!" Jesus replied, "seventy times seven!" (Matthew 18:21–22 TLB).

When the forgiveness piece finds its way to the table, it's time to pray first versus have an immediate conversation. The idea of forgiveness is easy to explain. The challenge is to follow through on what you know, and apply it to the relationship in the right way.

First of all, forgiveness is a choice. The definition of forgiveness is to cancel a debt. Christ's death on the cross canceled our sin debt. Therefore, as his followers, we are called to release others. Most Scriptures on forgiveness deal with an internal decision to let the person out of your system. This doesn't mean they will never have to own up to the offense. It also doesn't mean you have to stay their closest companion or even build a deeper relationship with them. If they are actually toxic, you may have to set firm boundaries, using what God is showing you to do. Forgiveness is between you and the Father. Just like you're leaning on him to help you say, *You hurt me, let's deal with this, I need you to understand,* you are also pulling upon his strength to cleanse your insides of the chant, *Hurt them, make them pay.*

This last part is the real kicker for Satan. Whenever the offender or the incident comes to mind—pray! Ask God's blessing on the offender. (Even if they're toxic, they still need prayer.) Also, ask him to help you see how the Holy Spirit worked in the incident and then give God the praise. This is not something done in the flesh or by one's own power. It's only possible as we continually pray, asking for the Holy Spirit's assistance. Then we can be an overcomer, delivered from unforgiveness (Isaiah 43:18, James 5:16).

If you still have lingering feelings or thoughts even after praying to God and your forgiveness feels insincere or phony, it may be time to talk with a Christian counselor, minister, or mature sister or brother in the faith. If you are still holding stuff over the head of the offender and waiting on them to talk with you and say they are sorry about the matter before you let it go, God is showing you a root of bitterness springing up. It's time to seek help outside of yourself.

Nothing is wasted with God. He can and will turn ashes to beauty, mourning into joy, and despair into praise (Isaiah 61:3).

Father, help me know when advice and conversations aren't in alignment with your will, so I may deal from a healthy place. Anything that has to do with you is healthy. Deliver me today, please! Deliver me from my past experiences. Make me whole today. Father, only you can make what was broken into a functioning element. So take control. Help me to be honest with others and myself. Remove the facade. Remove anything false. Check me! Check my heart! Remove jealousy, remove anger, remove bitterness. Search my heart and mind. If you find anything that is bad, cut it out! I'll undergo spiritual surgery to be spiritually healthy. Help me deal with my relationships from a secure place. Help me to be solid as a rock! In Jesus's name, amen.

Chapter 10

The Heart Matters

> My child, pay attention to what I say.
> Listen carefully to my words. Don't lose
> sight of them. Let them penetrate deep
> into your heart, for they bring life to those
> who find them, and healing to their whole
> body. Guard your heart above all else, for
> it determines the course of your life.
>
> **PROVERBS 4:20-23** NLT

In our physical body, the heart has everything to do with how the rest functions. Your spiritual heart is the same way. I remember someone reaching out to me saying, "The Lord is going to remove some people, but the impact will not be as tough." However, she later texted me, saying, "The Lord will be cleansing your heart." For some reason, her second message struck me because I thought

I was doing okay in my heart. I hadn't realized some things needed to be removed. And when I did an examination, the Holy Spirit revealed some heart issues. There were some defense mechanisms, old habits, and behaviors I'd learned over time or from previous experiences that were keeping me from progressing in my spiritual life. Sometimes our heart isn't necessarily dirty; it may be hardened from what has happened.

The Bible teaches us about a hardened heart. In some places, Scripture describes the heart as calloused. Some of our ways are motivated by our calloused hearts. One verse that always hits me is Matthew 13:15:

> For this people's heart has become calloused; they hardly hear with their ears, and they have closed their eyes. Otherwise, they might see with their eyes, hear with their ears, understand with their hearts, and turn, and I would heal them (NIV).

A callus is a thickened and hardened part of the skin or soft tissue. A callus doesn't happen overnight—it usually develops in an area where there's constant friction. When the Lord dealt with me about some hard places in my heart, he said, "It's due to the friction you've experienced." At times, people rub up against me the wrong way, or I rub up against them.

Usually, a callus is painful when it starts, and the pain you feel is your nerves warning you of the initial friction. For me, that soreness happens with shoes. I have a pair I love so much. They were *supposed* to be my comfortable option, but it quickly became clear they would not fit that purpose. I'm sure the same thing has happened to you! I adore those heels, but I quickly learned to always have a backup plan or another pair of shoes just in case.

Interestingly, I also have some quality shoes that are cute and flat, but they rub against the bone near my toes. Because they look good, I'd wear these shoes somewhat often. Not long after I got them, though, I noticed dark marks on my skin.

I like wearing my feet out during the summer, and these dark marks messed up my flow. So I attempted to narrow down which shoes they could be coming from so I could stop wearing them. I was in denial about my flats being the culprit because they were so cute, and I was hoping it could be another pair. But I was reminded of the pain and rubbing I ignored and then got used to the first few times I put on those flats. Because I hadn't stopped wearing them or done anything to protect that area of my skin, my body began building layers to protect itself from what I continued to allow.

This is how calluses develop in our hearts too. We naturally begin hardening ourselves as protection against pain and spiritual challenges. The Lord had me evaluate myself because sometimes I would stop after I saw dark marks forming in my life, but other times I would let it get to the calloused point. The dark marks show in our lives—in our attitudes, our ways of doing things, and in our responses.

I admire my mother's graceful disposition. She is always accepting and seasoned until she is disrespected. Then she immediately nips it in the bud with her raised eyebrows to signal, "Who are you talkin' to?" Or she will attempt to gain clarity before addressing what needs to be corrected. This reminds me to not automatically lash out in hopes of protecting myself, but to maintain my grace. We can't allow our calloused heart to make us react. Instead we have to take a beat and then respond.

What I'm getting at is this: Sometimes we act out of pain with people. Adding these layers of protection (calluses) to keep us from feeling what we should deal with overflows into our relationship with the Lord. The Holy Spirit may be speaking, "Soften up," or "Be a bit more gracious." But we push past and ignore the Spirit's little whispers because we have lost the ability to recognize the voice and prayerfully correct ourselves.

Matthew 13:15 references Isaiah 6:9–10, saying: "'Be ever hearing, but never understanding; be ever seeing, but never perceiving.' Make the heart of this people calloused; make their ears dull and close their eyes. Otherwise they might see with their eyes, hear with their ears, understand with their hearts, and turn and be healed" (NIV).

Many of the people God was addressing here were rebelling against what he was telling them through Isaiah, and God was ready to close them out of his promises if they didn't change. And since Jesus quotes it in the New Testament when he's talking about people not listening to him, we can be sure this warning applies to us too. It states that we "hardly hear" and have "closed our eyes." I can relate to this; I had an attitude when the Lord dealt with me concerning my heart. I was kind of like, *huh?* Baffled and confused. My ears and eyes were closed to what God's Spirit attempted to tell me.

Sometimes we can become so focused on other people's actions that we lose sight of our own role in how things play out—what's in our hearts that's carrying us to a place we don't intend to be and keeping us from connecting. Sometimes we are triggered by something that feels similar to something we dealt with in the past and respond the same way we did then, when in fact the situation is completely different and doesn't warrant that reaction. There are also times when things are not due to our hardened reactions or their hearts; it could instead be the Spirit driving us to uncover a truth that might not be pleasant to face. I know I've been challenged to live and see deeper.

Let's go back to the pair of shoes idea for a minute. Are there shoes you've worn that just don't fit? A pair you continue to grab from the closet despite the pain and continue to make excuses for so you can keep wearing them? Maybe the shoes looked cute on someone else, or when you saw them in an ad online or in a magazine, so you don't want to give them up. Or you told yourself they just have to be broken in a little bit longer. But they were never a good fit. Sometimes we must go through this process of elimination to see which shoes are not going to work. And just like we eventually need to toss those shoes, we need to toss out our past actions, ideas, and approaches so we can walk the paths we need to without harming ourselves and our hearts in the process.

I look at some of the documented horror stories out there, and I often pray, "Lord, don't let my heart go bad."

The next step in dealing with a callus is to pull back the layers of dead skin. Spiritually pulling back the layers little by little helps us deal with the root of our patterns and behaviors. This exercise helps us break cycles. Some layer questions to ask:

Did a traumatic event or painful loss happen? Did it cause you to lose faith in God?
Did another believer hurt or betray you?
Did you decide you could figure things out yourself?

A hardened, calloused heart causes a person to have difficulty perceiving or remembering things and dulls one's understanding, which means it may take a while for you to get through all the layers and finally get to the inital cause. Don't be discouraged!

Continuous, unrepentant sin (which includes thinking we have nothing to fix or be sorry for) causes the heart to turn cold and hard and can completely distance us from God (Romans 1:18–24)—so it's important for us to do the work.

Pride is another contributor to a calloused heart. In the Bible, King Nebuchadnezzar and the pharaoh of Egypt during Moses's time were two rulers who saw God's power but refused to bow the knee. They thought they could battle with the Almighty, True, and Living God, then declare victory—no way. God showed himself superior in each situation.

Unfortunately, this isn't something that happens just with unbelievers. Christians today can do the same. They insist on going their way and doing their own thing, thinking, *I can win. I know better than God.* Sometimes this is because they've been disappointed with God, or don't want to ask for forgiveness when they believe they're in the right. Human nature takes over. And in the end, they've become so used to the calluses building on their heart that those areas have spread and lost feeling, hardening to the point the Spirit can't find his way in.

To avoid this happening to us, we need to ask God for his searchlight. As David wrote in the psalms, "Search me, O God and know my heart. See if there is any offensive way in me, and lead me in the way everlasting" (Psalm 139:23–24 NIV). Once God shines that light, our job is to have the wisdom to recognize the problem so it can be repaired. (I realize my shoes are too tight or not fitting correctly; I can't wear them or there will be a problem.)

Repentance is the next item on the agenda—as is actually changing those spotlight things in our lives. (I was going in this direction, but now I've got to do a 360—get rid of the shoes that are causing the problem.)

Studying God's Word is a major factor in making sure we stay open to God's guidance. Don't simply read words—compare the way you're living to what God is saying. This keeps the friction to a minimum and prevents us from building up the same layers we just removed. It also reminds us of the right things our hearts should be letting in so they remain clean and open to change.

"How can a young [person] keep [their] way pure? By guarding it according to your word. With my whole heart I seek you; let me not wander from your commandments! I have stored up your word in my heart, that I might not sin against you" (Psalm 119:9–11).

Father, I thank you for working on me. Thank you for purifying my heart. Thank you for cleansing me of buildup from previous experiences. I understand my heart has to be in good condition so I can live the life you've called me to live. So today I ask that you have my heart beat as you call it. Heal me of any traumas that may cause me to feel triggered or attacked. I ask you to help me produce the fruits of the spirit—patience, understanding, and reasoning. Help me not to learn behaviors from TV, from my timeline, or from generational habits/behaviors. Please create in me a clean heart. Help me desire to be pure. I'd like to be genuine in all I do and say. Please help me. In Jesus's name, I pray, amen.

Cut It Out

> God, your God, will cut away the thick calluses
> on your heart and your children's hearts,
> freeing you to love God, your God, with your
> whole heart and soul and live, really live.
>
> ## DEUTERONOMY 30:6 MSG

When Jesus talked about hardened and calloused hearts in Matthew 13:15, it was not long after he'd been teaching his followers using parables, including the parable of the sower.

Back in Jesus's day, teachers used stories to tell their followers things they needed to understand, with the idea the story would make things easier to grasp. But because Jesus was a new kind of teacher—with a message that was often quite different from what the Jewish teachers were saying when it came to heavenly things—some people who came to hear Jesus speak didn't catch what he was saying. In fact, the disciples even asked Jesus why he kept telling parables when people often wound up confused.

Jesus's answer—that they needed to be healed in order to understand—has to do with how God works in our lives, as well as how we approach our relationship with him. Nothing God tells us is impossible to grasp. We simply have to be willing to listen and learn, or just like the hard earth in the parable of the sower, things will ping right off us no matter how close we think we're standing to Jesus. Or how often he throws the seeds at us.

The good news is that, unlike the people who listened to Jesus in his time, we have the benefit of the Holy Spirit's arrival, who can work on cutting away the callouses on our hearts from the inside, allowing us to truly understand what we need to know to live right. And God (through the Spirit) is very willing to remove those calluses if we only ask—he was even doing it way back in Deuteronomy when the hardhearted, we-know-better Israelites were mumbling and complaining in the desert. In many Bible translations, Deuteronomy 30:6 uses *circumcise your heart* or something similar. This phrase signals God wants to make a special covenant with us, where he helps us live our best life in exchange for our willingness to give him the power to remove the layers we've let build up—also freeing our minds and our hearts to love him in the pure and natural way we were made to. And that verse and promise also signal that no matter how stubborn or hardened we think we are, God can work with us and remove the evil and mess we've allowed to take over our hearts. Once that calloused part of us is gone, we'll also be less likely to want to go back to our old way of doing things.

I don't know about you, but I want to be able to hear what Jesus is saying and have that good life God is promising. So if you find yourself struggling with an issue in your heart—something you just can't let go of, something that keeps holding you back in your mind, or even something that is keeping you from really listening to those vibes and letting their seeds take root—ask God to help you cut it out.

Chapter 11

Keep Dreaming

> *Call to me and I will answer you,*
> *and will tell you great and hidden*
> *things that you have not known.*
>
> **JEREMIAH 33:3**

When I was around eighteen years old, I had a very vivid dream. I saw myself at the altar. I appeared smaller and weighed less, and a man in a blue suit and a little girl stood beside me. In this dream, my father had on the attire of a bishop, and he stood in front of us prophesying. I got the clear sense this was meant to represent me and my family, but in real life during this time, my father had yet to become a bishop, I wasn't married, and I didn't have any children.

I was dating someone at that time, but the picture I got of the man in my dream didn't match that person, and I knew it wasn't the guy I was dating even though I couldn't see the man's face. The little girl had light skin, with dark hair like my grandmother Mattie. The stature of the man in my dream is the same stature in my wedding photos today. It was Jordan! My husband appeared in my dream, but I didn't know it at the time.

So in this dream, there were two things happening. The Lord was showing me that my father would soon become a bishop. And I knew the man I was presently dating was not my future husband. But at the same time, the Lord showed me a glimpse of my future husband, and revealed I'd be happily married. While I think of this, it brings tears to my eyes. "Father, you were talking to me."

This dream happened ten to twelve years prior to me actually getting married—God revealed his plan to me as a young adult. Several times in the years before I started dating Jordan, my aunt Janet even came to me during revivals and said, "You don't know your husband yet." Which to me meant God continued to send reminders and signals connected to this part of my future.

I also remember having a conversation with my father while I was still discovering how the Lord was speaking to me. He explained that prophecy comes to us in the past, present, or future:

Past prophecies are things God (through his Spirit) showed us in the past, but the meaning of the prophecy isn't clear until later in our lives. These types of prophecies help us evaluate things that happen to us, since we can draw on what the Spirit showed us to guide us forward.

Present prophecies have to do with something happening in our lives right then that needs to be acted on.

Future prophecies are messages the Spirit sends that point to something that will happen later on—to us or possibly someone else.

Once I understood the three types, together these nuggets, these messages along the way, helped me unravel God's ways of speaking to me. And once I began having a lot of prophetic dreams, I began to study the dreamers in the Bible too.

Two of the most famous dreamers are Joseph and Daniel, who had a lot in common. Not only did both become high-ranking rulers after being brought to another country as captives, they were gifted dream-visions from God that came true. Joseph's visions were initially of the past variety and had to with his future profession and calling—where he saved people from famine and taught his brothers a big lesson along the way. I imagine those dreams helped him through a lot of cold nights in an Egyptian jail, when things definitely did not seem to be going his way! Daniel's most famous visions were in the far-future category; over many years, God showed him what would ultimately happen in the world leading up to and including the end times. Even now, people read the dreams Daniel wrote about and find truth in what he saw.

Daniel and Joseph were also gifted with a special ability when it came to dreams—they could sense when a dream came from God, whether it was their dream or someone else's dream. And in the cases where they were asked to interpret other people's dreams, the Bible notes they went to God for the answers, knowing they couldn't interpret anything on their own. And God came through in a major way—he helped Joseph interpret Pharaoh's dreams about cows and grain when no one else could, and Daniel was able to use the insight God sent to him to interpret a dream

King Nebuchadnezzar didn't even tell him about first, as well as give the meanings of many other important dreams while he served in Persia.

One dreamer not everyone thinks about is Jesus's earthly father, Joseph, because his present-tense dreams weren't as dazzling. But they were equally important for Joseph and very important for us, because if he hadn't listened, God's big, future plans would not have worked out the same way. Joseph's first recorded dream came shortly after he found out Mary was pregnant. Because this was the first and only virgin pregnancy, it's understandable that Joseph didn't believe Mary was carrying God's child, and he'd decided to divorce Mary (engagement was legally close to marriage in their culture). But then an angel appeared to Joseph while he was asleep and told him Mary was telling the truth. Joseph could've dismissed the dream and kept looking at Mary sideways like everyone else, but the Bible tells us Joseph accepted everything the dream said as soon as he woke up, apparently without further questions. That reaction and his faith are really amazing when you think about them.

And Joseph's amazing dream reactions don't end there. After Jesus was born, Joseph, Mary, and Jesus moved into a house in Bethlehem. When the wise men arrived at their house one day bearing gifts, it was probably a celebratory time for the family. But while Joseph slept that night, an angel told him to run to Egypt because King Herod saw Jesus as a threat to his kingdom and was planning to kill him. The Bible says that after waking up, Joseph quickly packed up his family and headed to Egypt. Not long after the family left, Herod started killing any boys under two years old in Bethlehem. Later, God sent Joseph two more dreams—one telling him it was now safe to head back to Israel with Jesus and

Mary because Herod had died, and another soon after telling them to settle in Nazareth so Jesus would be safe from Herod's replacement. Which not only saved Jesus's life, it put him exactly where he needed to be according to the prophecies.

When we read these stories and others in the Bible like them, we might think, "Well, God singled these people out because they were special somehow" or "That wouldn't happen today." But when you read each person's full story in the Bible, it becomes clearer that most dreamers in Scripture were seen as farmers, students, and everyday people until they decided to listen to what God was sending and their lives shifted. For example, while the two Josephs and Daniel did have some big dreams, they started out their lives and faith journeys like a lot of us—they simply grew into good dream-listeners and learned what to do with what they dreamed because they put in spiritual work. And because God still can and does send past, future, and present dreams to his people today, it means we can look to their examples and learn how to grow to a place we can better understand what God is sending. A lot of it comes down to having a solid faith and learning to listen. With Old Testament Joseph, he likely didn't fully grow into his spiritual maturity until he got to Egypt—he was bragging about his dreams before he understood what they fully meant—but once he became humble and understood how to rely on God, he knew to wait for clarity on each dream before he acted or gave advice. Daniel appears to be a little more solid in his faith in comparison when we first meet him. Daniel 1:17 tells us his gift for "understanding in all visions and dreams" came from God after he took a stand and refused to eat food God had told him was unclean, but one key to that gift was likely also Daniel's commitment to always stay connected to God in prayer; things were clearer because he knew the vison-giver's voice. And while we don't know much about Joseph from the New Testament, he is described as a faithful man who tried to follow God's law in his life, and his actions show us he was someone who had simply learned to trust based on what he knew about God, even when a message came with big life challenges. What we can take away from all these biblical examples is the idea that when we commit to developing our relationship with God, he is more able to speak to us through dreams when needed—and our faith and growing understanding of who God is can help us recognize what he shows us and have more confidence to move once we know the answers.

But how do we know if *God* is sending us dream messages?

The Lord had to show me how to tell the difference between prophetic dreams and dreams that come from eating Flaming Hot Cheetos before bed. I've come to know a dream is from the Lord because of the vibe and the feeling I have *after* the dream: I have a sense of security. I feel sure about my dream, without questions. Following the dream, I experience stillness.

I also learned how to determine when the Lord is speaking to me through a dream because of a conversation I had with a friend who has since passed away. Before her death, she experienced the same kind of prophetic dreaming I do. I'll never forget it. She said, "I know the Lord is speaking to me because I always remember that dream. The dreams I forget are not from the Lord." What God has emphasized for me since is a dream from the Lord is one I will remember vividly—weeks, even years, later.

I have those dreams where I think to myself, "This is really good. I wanna go back to sleep and get back to my dream." But I don't remember many of those later. So when one stays with me, stays on my mind, lives in color, I know I need to pay attention.

Psychologists who study dreams don't know for sure why we forget a lot of our dreams, remember others, or even why we have certain dreams over and over. But as they've continued to study dreaming, they've come to believe the things our brains and bodies go through are necessary for us to function correctly, or can be signs of our emotional well-being. That might all be true—and some of it lines up with what we've been looking at in a way—however, I've also learned there's definitely a difference scientifically and spiritually when it comes to dreaming and what dreams mean for our lives.

I remember being in a hotel room and there being a dark cloud in the sky in a bodily form. The hotel was in a small town and the room was very dark. I remember there being old rusty greens and blue undertones to the room. It felt very horror movie-ish because of the wooden furniture and old floral wallpaper. I didn't like it the moment I walked in. There were two parts to the room, a sitting area and bedroom, and not long after I got in I had placed my suitcase on a wooden coffee table and gone to lie down in the bedroom part. When I woke up from a nap, I lay there for a minute and soon realized I couldn't get up or speak, but I was able to see everything. I saw a spider coming toward me.

Science says that this was sleep paralysis—my brain shutting my body down to protect me after a bad dream—but I had more than just a scientific encounter. This was a spiritual encounter. I wasn't able to move or speak until I tried saying, "The blood of Jesus!" I remember my mother telling me, "When you can't do anything else, call 'Jesus' or plead the blood of Jesus!" I thought it with my mind and then it came through my lips. Finally, I came out of the paralysis with deep breathing, a full revival all alone, and the spider disappeared. Like it had shriveled up into the wood of the ceiling.

I was too embarrassed to share this at the time, but the enemy wrestled with me and showed me what he wanted from me. I kept praying and cried out to the Lord and asked him to keep me covered.

I traveled with my friend Cyndy at this time and finally told her what I'd experienced. She didn't seem surprised and never made me feel like an oddball. She just covered me with prayer. The enemy wanted my voice and my mobility but did not get it.

A few years later, I had a dream about a woman in church, who appeared as a witch. She disguised herself as a church lady, but she kept her black-gloved hand over my mouth. I couldn't get her off of me. As I dug deeper, the enemy tried fighting me to keep me quiet. As I unpacked everything later, I realized I often felt like I said too much when I said just the right thing. It's important knowing the difference between when the Holy Spirit is convicting you and when the adversary, or yourself, is condemning you.

I share this story because I've noticed over time we've become relaxed on spirituality and warfare.

God can use our dreams to communicate with us, but the enemy can also attempt to use them as well. He's out to cause us to fear and to not move forward in God's plans and purposes for our lives.

Obviously, I still believe the Lord speaks to me, to us, through dreams. But I'm also giving a stiff warning—be careful. Be discerning. Not every dream and vision is from God. I believe you can lead yourself into some dark places if you attempt to analyze every one of your dreams. Especially if you are not spending time in devotions, studying the Bible, or going to God in prayer as part of the analysis. (Remember our biblical examples.) Just waiting on a dream for God to communicate with you? No!

God's primary way of speaking to us is through the Bible. God never separates himself from his written word. If the dream is contrary to the principles in the Scriptures, this dream is not from God.

If you have a dream that stays with you, it is bothering you for a reason. Here are some practical steps for understanding. Pray, pray, pray. Ask the Holy Spirit for wisdom. Stay in the Word and ask for guidance there as you study. Ask a seasoned saint, a pastor, your spiritual mentor, or someone you trust (who walks with the Lord) about your dream. Finally, if the Father seems to be asking you to do something or continue to do something—do it! It may seem impossible but step out in faith. God works through our circumstances to confirm his messages to us. I believe our lives can be filled with wonders, miracles, and mysteries from the Lord. But once again, be prayerful and discerning.

Prayer

Numbers 12:6 says, "Hear my words: If there is a prophet among you, I the LORD make myself known to him in a vision; I speak with him in a dream." I know you can do the same in me. So, today, if there's a gift for me to see in dreams, I ask that you anoint me with clarity so I know how to apply it to my life. I ask that you help me follow 1 John 4:1 and test what I feel, helping me to know which dreams are from you. Thank you for trusting me with the gift to see. Help me forget the dreams that don't mean anything, but allow me to vividly remember any from heaven. I come against nightmares and tormenting spirits that may try to visit me. I ask that you, God, remove any ill-motivated forces. As I sleep, it is one of the most vulnerable times in my day. So please protect me as I sleep and rest all parts of my being. I denounce any interruption that might stop the flow of any heaven-bound encounters with you. And while you grow me up in the Spirit and with spiritual gifts, please keep me clothed with humility so I always stand in awe of you. I declare you will forever be my God and no self-righteousness will swallow me up, Your answers and mysteries are revealed to me, but I am forever your servant. In Jesus's name, amen!

Chapter 12

Baggage

*Point out anything in me that offends you,
and lead me along the path of everlasting life.*

PSALM 139:24 NLT

I was left out of a lot of things while in my late teens through my mid-twenties, even though I thought I was the central connection between a few of my friends. Some of my peers wouldn't invite me to certain gatherings because we didn't have the same mentality. The way I saw it, I wanted to use discretion when it came to the things I did while growing and exploring, and they wanted to live for the moment. As a result, it seemed they thought certain activities were not "appropriate" for me to attend.

I had to find out about fun events from pictures on social media or by word of mouth—along with everyone else. I remember seeing some of the guys I had dated in a few of the photos, and no one in my circle had even told me they'd been hanging out together. It felt like an "everybody keeps it from Ki" kind of thing. I was definitely in a space of taking nearly everything personally. Especially when I found out some of the people I called friends were associating with my exes, and everyone knew but me.

Over time, I found myself picking up vibes. Vibes that they didn't care about my feelings at all. That I wasn't welcome because I might ruin their good time. That we'd never really been friends, and they'd been using me to get the connections they wanted. All of this made me feel like all those relationships had been an act instead of something real. As those vibes started growing and getting into my heart, they started affecting every part of my life, from the circle I kept to how I evaluated the world . . . and how I saw myself.

This whole situation often left me hanging out with my parents, grandparents, and brother, as well as the one or two trusted friends. I wanted to stay where I felt safe, considered, and included. For a while, I didn't understand why I didn't have those things in my life. Why almost everyone around me—even those I called friends—would treat me so poorly. So, at a young age, while I *knew* everyone, I *felt* alone. Being a pastor's kid and having a public responsibility of my own thanks to my music career, I was forced to learn relational wisdom and compartmentalization at a young age—how to interact with people and not let others' behavior affect what I was hoping to achieve. With time, I grew to identify what I was missing in friendship and loyalty, and how I kept looking for those things in the wrong places. As a result, I began finding deeper connections with older people.

One day, I had a conversation with Momma. I think she felt my pain. She gave me some simple, straightforward advice: "Move on! You do your thing and let them do theirs. When it's time for y'all to do life together, go if you want to, and if you don't, that's okay! If they don't, that's okay too."

I also remember sitting at the dinner table with my grandfather around this same time. I shared with him how I felt, and he shared another simple thought: "You're doing fine if you only have two friends." But I wanted more friends! I also wanted more from my grandfather on this subject. His one sentence was all I got. He noticed the question on my face that said, "That's it?" However, when I reflected on their words later, I realized these conversations meant the most in my life at this point.

Every lesson from them helps me understand life now. As a result of their advice, I talked with seasoned people about the connections I wanted to share with my peers and how to make those connections. While I kept getting good advice that pointed me toward seeking solid and meaningful relationships over many friends, I didn't want to seem weird or like an old soul during this process, so I still held on to my old mindset and included people who didn't include me, thinking that keeping them in my loop would convince them to connect with me in a different way. But over time, I realized there was no point in spending money and celebrating with folks who continued to be limited with me when it came to our relationships. I couldn't avoid the truth any longer. So I stopped having birthday parties or other events. I just hung around my family and older friends or made work my focus.

Even though I thought I was maturing and moving past my issues, I began carrying these memories of broken relationships and deep feelings of neglect through my life. Until I bumped into friends who shared very similar sentiments—about me. As we started to break things down together, I realized that for years I'd dealt with my old friends based on who they'd been in the past. And just like I felt they had changed in ways that made them feel distant to me, in their minds I had changed too. To them, I came off as acting "funny" or critical when we were together, when it was actually me figuring out how I felt about certain people in that moment. I was trying to learn how to navigate the shifts we were having in the relationship.

It was like I didn't know whether to give too much, to give very little, or to give nothing at all. I was learning boundaries, and how to courteously express myself. They were feeling the vibe of me not feeling them, and I was picking up on what they were feeling toward me. As a result, I carried this bad vibe with me and kept projecting these old feelings and assumptions onto new people I met.

I definitely carried around that unacknowledged emotional baggage from previous experiences and relationships for a while afterward. It was like I was taking the same old luggage to new places, never unpacking it or even opening it up. And by making that old baggage such a big part of my journey, I wasn't giving anyone a chance or the benefit of the doubt. I kept shutting out new people with pure intentions, people I could have truly connected with.

My feelings of anger, shame, distrust, and rejection needed to be taken out, examined, cleaned, or discarded. I was able to explore some of these feelings once I did what Momma said—"Do my thing"—and started navigating life and new relationships. But there were others I wasn't ready to address until I began sharing with some of the old friends who hadn't included me, letting them know how I felt.

I asked some of my peers, "Why wasn't I invited?" We began

defining the relationships and the tables turned. Conversations with them helped me fully understand our different perspectives and to see that they were growing too—I wasn't the only one trying to figure things out. My imagination had left me with, "They didn't want me there" or focused on, "This is the way I would've handled it." Our talks showed it wasn't that simple— that there had been unintended hurts on both sides as we'd all started finding our different paths. And while others respected the life I was trying to live and the public figure I was called to be, they didn't want me at their events because of how far our paths had diverged. In the end, it all boiled down to maturity levels and relational maintenance. Are we in the same place in life to make this work, and do we want to do the work to keep the relationship together in the future? Or do we come to an agreement that the vibes are leading us to amicably part ways?

This is a point where the Spirit really started opening my eyes and helping me see what my vibes were telling me—that I needed to stop stubbornly holding on to the past and learn from the experience, and then move on to friendships that would benefit me and help me thrive. I also had to fully listen to the advice I'd been getting, which I now see was sent to me from a spiritual place. Friendships worth hanging on to are ones that come with a healthy balance and respect, as well as support and joy. Like 1 Thessalonians 5:11 tells us, "Therefore encourage one another and build one another up." In fact, one way you can tap into the Spirit's guidance is by looking at what the Bible has to say and filtering your relationships through that lens—since the Bible is the way God communicates with us most often. (If you need some verses to get started, check out Romans 12:10; Proverbs 16:28 and 18:24; and John 15:13–15.) The Bible also helps us see the signs of a bad relationship—like one that keeps secrets, spreads lies, and keeps doing things that hurt you. (See Proverbs 17:9 and 22:24–25; Job 16:14; and 1 Corinthians 15:33.) There might even be times the unction we looked at earlier comes into play—you might overhear some wise words and even come across a TV episode that make you look at what is happening in your life in a new way, because God knew it was the message you needed to hear.

As I looked at how I'd been approaching my relationships, I also discovered I had begun living my life out of spite rather than growth. When Momma told me I shouldn't put my life on hold due to others not including me, she was not suggesting I become a bitter woman. So I had to remove bitterness and spite from my emotional baggage too.

This led me to do a heart check. I started journaling how I felt. Some of the things I reflected on were current seasons that needed to be addressed, and some were in the past and needed to be left behind. Some relationships are meant to end. In the fall, leaves naturally fall from trees so new ones can grow. Once I established I was in that season, the discovery of seasonal connections was the highlight for me for some time.

However, I had to strengthen my relationship with myself for these lessons to last a lifetime. That self-connection was what was missing. I was so concerned with committing to relationships with everyone else, I'd forgotten how to commit to myself. Meanwhile, I didn't consider how I am the next person's teacher, or think about how I should be treated. This level of soul-searching led me to a lot of discoveries about what I decided to put up with and how it was needlessly adding to my bitterness and frustration. It also helped me understand what I needed to look for in others—what

I needed to truly complement me and help me grow, as well as challenge and support me in my journey.

Another thing that became clear as I worked on my self-relationship was that to keep everything in check inside, a close relationship between me and the Father cannot be on a seasonal basis. There were some things I needed to address with the Father. A lot of those internal conversations went along the lines of, "What we're not going to do is have ourselves a pity party. We must acknowledge how we're feeling to explore solutions, but also move forward with prayer and supplication to sift through and assess." The moving forward with God's help is key. I think about the apostle Paul, who had a dramatic spiritual conversion and went from murdering Christians to sharing the gospel. He knew a lot about having to get past old thoughts and behaviors. He spoke confidently about "forgetting what is behind" (Philippians 3:13 NIV). In other words, don't look back! No time to dwell on past issues. Anything that is hindering you from moving forward needs to be addressed.

And to move forward, it's essential to judge how you're feeling through that higher, heavenly lens. See if the reaction is reasonably justified. While feelings are never right or wrong, the way you choose to react to something isn't always right. What's the vibe you get when you take a moment to really listen to the voice inside you, instead of focusing on what you *want* it to say? Sometimes our imaginations create a whole situation that never existed. Sometimes they'll lead us to feel things we shouldn't. When we only consult with ourselves and stay in our minds, we may say the wrong things. Emotions aren't always dependable guides. That is why it's important to pray about everything (see Philippians 4:6–7).

What we *feel* is real. But we must be responsible and deal with how we feel. Sometimes dealing with it means processing it with others, getting a different perspective that helps us clear up the vibes. I've had to remember that no one is obligated to be on my side, but they should tell me the truth so I can do what is just. (This is also the sign of a good relationship—honest support.) Then there are times it's necessary to process our feelings within ourselves. This is also healthy. We *know* what's fair—to us and to others. And to be honest, as soon as you feel your personal interpretations taking hold, it's time to sit down and work through what is true and what is only your feelings. If we desire to truly please the Lord, then the Holy Spirit will assist us when it comes to sifting through our emotions.

Have you ever gotten a stack of mail and packages to sift through? To me, emotions are like that mail, and the circumstances that bring about those emotions are like the people who deliver the mail. Sometimes the mail person comes gently and takes their time to make sure everything arrives safely. Sometimes they throw mail at your doorstep, not concerned about what's in the package because they're just interested in making it to the next drop. So when you suddenly feel "some kind of way," it might be the way your internal "mail system" is delivering your emotions.

Sometimes we accidentally get the wrong mail too. Have you ever opened an envelope or package and started looking inside before realizing it wasn't addressed to you? I've done this and then panicked from looking at a bill that didn't belong to me. It was a neighbor's! Once I read it, I said, "This ain't mine!" In a similar way, what feelings have you experienced that don't belong to you? What thoughts have you entertained that were actually an adversary's suggestions? Sometimes you have to respond strongly when it's dropped on you, "This ain't mine!" You don't have to accept all mail as valid communication. That's why it's essential to look at the address, be clear of your identity, and make sure the delivery was sent to the right recipient. After verifying the address, see that you read carefully, or else your emotions will drive you into a frenzy.

We'll talk more about emotions in later chapters, but remember: When our emotions drive our lives, we must take our rightful positions by choosing to not make everything a "thing." We are to be driven by God's Spirit, grow in the Lord, and allow him to help us interpret the unspoken (see John 16:13).

When it comes to relationships, some of our experiences have everything to do with what we needed to go through to learn a higher truth. For example, consider the lessons you have learned from the past that can be applied in the present. God is always on your side. I have learned that focusing on the vibe of offense can cause us to hold on to rocks and miss the diamonds in the rough in friendships and other close relationships, and also miss the opportunities to grow and move closer to the good friend we're called to be as well.

Prayer

Father, thank you for delivering me from past experiences. Thank you for removing the emotional baggage and dead weight that would have caused me to move forward as a non-spiritual being. Help me to clear out anything that is hindering me from moving forward in your eyes. I speak understanding over my life. I ask for constant revelations in the major and minor things in my life that help me progress in the way you desire. God, I ask that you work alongside me so I am sure of the vibes I'm feeling. Let me be so intertwined with you that your Spirit overrides my unwarranted feelings. Father, you have full reign in my judgment. Assess, sift, and examine with me. Heal me of any unspoken or unresolved traumas, so I can operate as a healthy heir of your mission. Remove all emotional and mental sickness. I plead the blood of Jesus over my life. Help me deal with others gently and as you would. Help me extend grace and forgiveness. Help me know when the season is up. Remind me of the blessings that are mine for a lifetime. In Jesus's name, amen.

Chapter 13

Who's All Over There?

> For at one time you were darkness, but now
> you are light in the Lord. Walk as children
> of light (for the fruit of light is found in all
> that is good and right and true), and try
> to discern what is pleasing to the Lord.
>
> **EPHESIANS 5:8-10**

When I am invited to an event, I'll usually ask, "Who's all going?"
And if it's a get-together at someone's house, I'll ask, "Who's all
over there?" Some of my family and friends ask the same question
when I send an invitation to them. It's our way of ensuring we are
on our best behavior so we'll contribute to a good time, making
sure there's no one there we're not ready to see, or just examining
the place before going so we're prepared.

When we are around certain people, we get a vibe, good or

bad. And that can affect our behavior. But like we discussed earlier, we can't just go with what we think is right when it comes to a relationship or a situation. We need to deeply listen to the vibe and determine if it's leading us to communion and connection with that person for some reason, or if it is calling us to step away because it's not the time or place for a meeting to happen.

When we are honest with ourselves and realize the signals we're getting are signs we're not in a good place, or are led to see the location is not a good place for us to be, we may take a raincheck on a date and decide to be selfless to ensure our loved ones can enjoy themselves. Or that we don't put ourselves in a situation that could be harmful for us or someone else. Does that mean this should always be our approach? No. As kingdom citizens, it is our duty to grow in the Lord, to allow the Holy Spirit to help us so that we can learn to be with others and stay supportive of our loved ones when they have invited us. Sometimes that's what the vibes are for—to give us the notices we need to shift and mature, so the next time we're in that situation we are spiritually ready and can receive the invitation with a positive feel. (The same is true for others—if someone else isn't in a good place to see us, we might get the vibe we need to keep our distance until the timing is right.)

That growing maturity also has to do with accepting what a vibe is actually telling us—learning to discern a real call for us to stay away at that time from what is simply our discomfort or desire to avoid something or someone we don't want to face. Especially when the vibe is telling us it's something we do need to take on or get past.

I've had to consider, when choosing not to attend certain gatherings with relatives or friends, "How does my absence make them feel?" It is required of us to love our neighbors even when we don't agree. The Lord convicted me and said, "You can't let your feelings drive you." I need to live by this Scripture: "Forgive each other because the Lord forgave you. Do all these things; but most important, love each other . . . Let the peace that Christ gives CONTROL your thinking, because you were all called together in one body to have peace" (Colossians 3:13–15 ICB, emphasis mine).

It is understood, some people have different morals, backgrounds, and perspectives. Everyone may not mesh well together. Uncomfortable things happen. Is this saying, "Ignore how you feel"? No. It is saying be prayerful about all of your actions. The urge not to go could be the Holy Spirit saying, "Sit this one out," but it might also be the Spirit telling you it's an opportunity to go and see others in a different light, where the discomfort is a warning you need to go in carefully. The only way to tell is to sit with the vibe and unpack it, including praying over it when you feel torn. It also helps to ask for strength and guidance once you know you're being led to go out of your place of comfort and into something that could be difficult. Our standards face challenges as we learn from one another and broaden our perspectives. On these occasions, misunderstandings can arise due to a lack of communication, bad gossip, or misinterpretations if we go in with the wrong mindset and preparation. On the other hand, if we have it in our hearts to give others a chance and truly listen, great connections can and do happen, and we may learn more about someone's depth once we truly interact.

The Lord has really worked on me. As I discussed before, I was always ready to read, release, and cut off certain people . . . until I understood that one of the most sacred traditions in Christianity is communion. Communion in the church has everything to do with remembering the body and blood of Jesus Christ, so we're connecting with the promises God gives us and committing to living like Christ. It can also be defined as having a deep connection with another person, one where you can share things on a personal and spiritual level. When we enter this type of personal communion, we then begin to grow. We learn why we do things the way we do, say what we say, or act the way we act. Since we all come from different homes and experiences, we obviously don't share the same parents, ideas on how things should be (because of how we grew up), or ways of approaching things based on where we live or our cultural traditions. Our lessons and training might've been a bit different, and that's okay. When we get together, it is an opportunity to maturely grow together.

I think it's safe to say, some of us prefer keeping up an easygoing atmosphere rather than having to deal with the weight of an elephant in the room. Let's dive into that phrase, "the elephant in the room." Actually consider the weight of one of the largest animals on earth. What if an elephant was still its physical size but didn't have the same weight? It could easily be moved. So the weight of the elephant (the issue) is what should be considered. The "weight" is invisible. The thought that adds to the heft is invisible. The vibe that causes us to feel uncomfortable with that elephant's heavy presence is invisible. But the actual weight of the elephant is real and pressing, and it could be deadly or life-altering. Sometimes we don't see the issue or really understand it, but we can *feel* it. And please believe you're not the only one feeling it or seeing it.

We're called to remove all the weights that are holding us back from growing personally and spiritually into who we're called to be (see Hebrews 12:1), and to enjoy a free atmosphere that lets us move forward. Sometimes certain weights (issues) appear in the place we're gathering with others so we can resolve it and free ourselves. But to do that, it takes everyone working as one to acknowledge the elephant we're dealing with. That's why considering "who is in the room" or "who is going to be there" is necessary. Some people aren't interested in playing a part in removing the heaviness that is weighing on us. Some may even enjoy the weight that lingers and grows after we leave the room. Have you ever seen a disturbing post in your social media feed, and then notice in the comment section, "I'm just waiting on the comments . . ."? Some people enjoy mess.

In those cases, you need to address the weight, but rely on the vibe to show you the time and the place.

Also, a truth to admit is that it takes a certain amount of energy to "put on" around others if you're really feeling heavy. You don't know what to say. You worry if you've said too much, and agonize over whether it was said wrong or said to the right person. Not all of us have learned to be diplomatic and not allow others to control us. Sometimes the question of "who all will be there?" is not only to excuse our absence, but to prepare ourselves mentally and spiritually for certain individuals in the room.

A last thing to consider is, will you be too busy with the people and the event to be able to listen to the Holy Spirit's guidance? When we ask the question, and ask our spiritual assessors, it helps us to consider everything. The Holy Spirit will do this with you and for you, and will teach you if you make yourself available no matter who is around or what is happening around you.

Prayer

Father, I ask that you anoint me so I can be clear in every situation I walk into. Help me discern and assess prior to my attendance to ensure I am not entangling myself in a situation that isn't authorized by you. I understand that as I grow there will be choices you will protect me from, and some things will happen that are out of my control. However, I thank you for giving me peace and direction, and for covering me when I make mistakes. I will not allow my mistakes to hinder me, nor will I use them as a crutch. Today, I ask that you allow me to be mature in the Spirit to ensure I am assessing all things alongside the Holy Spirit. Give me the peace to not feel guilty when asking "who's all over there." Be my spiritual ears when hearing names, to note the depths of the environment I may walk into. If it will be a gossiping session, put hesitancy in my spirit. If it is not part of your predestined plan, allow me to get there too late. Help me know when it's time to leave and when it's time to stay. I understand this prayer may also put me in the hot seat at times, because you'll be leading me into interactions I would have avoided before, but I ask that you're with me while sitting there to handle it with victory and not defeat. Remove guilt from my back when deciding to not go. Convict me when I've given too many rainchecks and when I've given too much. In Jesus's name, amen.

Chapter 14

Solo Dolo

> *Then, because so many people were coming and going that they did not even have a chance to eat, [Jesus] said to them, "Come with me by yourselves to a quiet place and get some rest."*
>
> **MARK 6:31** NIV

I remember when I was young, I always had to do things in packs. I had to go to the restroom with a friend, dine out with a friend, or go to the movies with a friend. Until I began seeing my own company as enjoyable and started doing things on my own. This type of comfortable being-alone time is called "solo dolo."

Interestingly, when I first started going out on my own, I thought I needed to actually do things to occupy myself so people didn't look at me funny. Then I realized there were others who did things by themselves too—and they weren't doing anything big.

What really helped me push past the awkward thought of being out by myself was when I began people watching and enjoying nature rather than feeling the need to fill my time in conversation. It was like I took a girdle off. When we're around people, we are so used to compression and needing to fit a space, but when we are solo alongside the Holy Spirit, we can breathe differently.

When I began to go solo, my mind would wander and my attention shifted. I began saying, "Thank you, Lord." This welcomed the Holy Spirit into my space. I turned out to be pretty dope company, and this new companion—the Holy Spirit—turned out to be even cooler. Without distractions, I was able to filter out wrong thoughts when I went off by myself, and I began to see how busy I was doing life but not doing purpose. As a result, I also began seeing the beauty in having lunch by myself or driving alone. These became moments when the Holy Spirit assured me I *wasn't* alone. I realized I'd gotten so used to filling my time with what my peers wanted to do and what our culture wanted me to focus on, I hadn't given God enough time to make himself heard.

Sometimes the Holy Spirit will lead us into a time of aloneness, solitude. This can prove to be very valuable, refreshing, and insightful. We need to get out of the public eye, or out of the way of people's opinions and criticisms. This time alone should be a time to connect with God's voice.

I remember being in a plane for longer than the predicted flight time. The pilot came on and made the announcement, "There is too much traffic to land and the weather is too bad." So we were in the sky for three hours—instead of one—where there was less traffic circling around. This is when the Lord spoke to me and said, "Sometimes I can't find a landing space with you because there's too much traffic." Sometimes too much traffic crowds your mental space, and can drown out the still voice of the Holy Spirit. Having moments to yourself isn't only good for you, it's refreshing to the soul. Self-care isn't always about being selfish.

Some of God's greatest leaders gladly took alone time. Jesus and Elijah were two people who sought out solitude. And who better to measure ourselves with than Jesus? Jesus went solo dolo when he was in preparation for something major, like the start of his ministry (Luke 4:1–2, 12–15), when he needed a break between big events with his followers (Mark 6:30–32), when he needed prayer time (Mark 1:35), when he was processing sadness or grief (Matthew 14:1–13), and before making big decisions (Luke 6:12–13).

Elijah spent time in isolation during his ministry to the people of Israel, often after very difficult moments. Just before one of these instances, Elijah had appeared on the scene to confront King Ahab and Queen Jezebel and their prophets of the false god Baal. He put on an impressive demonstration using a sacrifice that proved to the people watching that God was more powerful than Baal—and Elijah looked like a very confident prophet throughout, heckling the Baal worshipers and creating an altar so impossible to light that only God could have done it. But after this great victory (1 Kings 18:17–40), Jezebel, an avid Baal worshiper, threatened Elijah's life, and Elijah immediately got scared and ran away.

He found himself in a cave, filled with fear, a wavering faith, and depression. The prophet was so emotionally distraught and worn at this point, he told God, "Just kill me" (see 1 Kings 19:4). Instead of fulfilling the prophet's request, though, God personally came to Elijah in a whisper, then refreshed his servant with food, water, and sleep.

God used isolation in Elijah's life to personally address his needs and to give him the power to do what he needed to in his ministry (right after resting and eating the food God gave him, Elijah spent forty days doing tasks God told him to perform). For me, after a time of isolation and reflection, I come out more focused and ready and less annoyed by what someone might say. I take what I need from conversations and move on rather than taking everything and focusing on the negatives. As we evolve as good people managers and learn to use isolation to refresh and refine ourselves, common annoyances are no longer triggers for us but instead work as gentle notes. They no longer weigh us down, and we learn not to move based off knowledge that is "fake" versus "wise," because we stepped away to develop ourselves and our inner senses. Our peace becomes steady, and over time we are unable to be moved by people and their actions and more able to go into strategizing that benefits us and what we're called to do.

But remember, while taking some solo dolo is needed, it's not healthy to stay in isolation forever. God designed us to be with people, not living on a deserted island. If we stay away for too long, we'll miss out on life, answers, and the outside replenishment being with wise people can bring. In isolation, we only have ourselves to reason with. If we spend too much time in that one-track loop, we lose the opportunity to gain other perspectives and broaden our ways of thinking, and receive less of a refresh as a result. Allowing other perspectives into our lives, from safe people, after filtering out the noise, broadens our bandwidth for dealing with people and gives us more understanding to pull from when the next break is due.

*Thank you, Lord, for loving me enough to take away
the spirit of heaviness. I remove that garment and trade
it with you for joy (Matthew 11:28–29). Today, I ask
that you continue to reassure me that being alone doesn't
mean I am lonely, and that even if I'm alone physically
you're always with me. Thank you for the awakening
conversations you've had with me. Thank you for this
season of maturation. You're helping me choose wisely,
and I understand that when I am simply thirsty for you, I
say yes to the right companionship that resembles you and
not my anxious desire for company. I enjoy the time away
with you. I acknowledge that these moments of being alone
are not an excuse to avoid people because you take joy in
relationships. So, today I'm learning balance when it comes
to your guidance and truth. Alone time with you allows me
to hear my thoughts and to filter them with your guidance.
So, today I bask in the things you've done on earth and seek
time with you and rolling solo dolo. Amen.*

Chapter 15

Who's Who?

> *Behold, how good and pleasant it is*
> *when brothers dwell in unity!*
>
> **PSALM 133:1**

The Holy Spirit desires to be involved in every part of our lives now and in the future. That includes who we invite over, where we are working, where we're schooling, who we are dating, who we'll marry, how we'll advise our children, and so much more. God distributes angels, or agents, in your life to help you manage these parts of your life.

Family is probably one that is most present, as they know you well and can help you reflect on all the different parts of your life. And odds are, at least some family will always be part of your life. The people I'm related to, I can't get rid of them, and they can't get rid of me even if they wanted to—*we's related, y'all!* The connection is by blood. The connection is permanent and can't be changed.

I often contrast family relationships and other permanent connections with casual or seasonal relationships. Seasonal connections are those that can make a difference, but your time together is meant to be short. Maybe you work on a project together. When it's done, it's "See ya," but conversations or experiences often linger and shape you during that time. Or maybe it's a relationship you outgrow over time, or even one you can return to from time to time but it never goes very deep. No matter how they come about or how long they last, these relationships are still ordained and designed by God. Each relationship you have carries a lesson or purpose.

When I wasn't in sync with the Holy Spirit, I tried making my seasonal relationships turn into lifetime relationships. Can a seasonal relationship become a long-term friendship? Yes! However, it's important we seek the Lord's advice on where we are going with our connections to ensure we aren't unnecessarily hurt.

Growing up, my mother was always so on point when it came to my seasonal relationships. She was my guardian angel. She quickly discerned who was there to stay and who wasn't. The Lord has used my mother to help me see relational value. She has also helped me see how the Holy Spirit guides us to be the best we can be in relationships.

Something I often ask is, could this person be in my life to help push me, or so I push them into the next phase of life? Where I'm a pedestal for you, and you are a pedestal for me? Or could it be a relationship where the two of us will be making deposits or withdrawals—where one takes, the other gives, and the balances on both sides don't equal out. As bad as it sounds, relationships like this, which don't seem mutually beneficial at the time, are a thing. It's one reason I've gotten frustrated with some connections I've had—the transactions failed to be mutual. But eventually the Holy Spirit helped me realize that sometimes *The assignment is for you to pour.* Or I've been shown I'm someone's assignment, and so I just need to take in what is being offered. Once I realized this, the purpose and timeline of the relationship was clearer.

These questions and assessments using the Spirit as a guide have helped me recognize the power and presence of lifetime friendships and besties. These are the people vested in us, who really care about our well-being. There is a mutual connection, a covenant. We get the strong sense we are meant to be in each other's lives, even if we can't explain it.

"Soul sister" isn't just a phrase; friends can truly be connected by the Spirit. David and Jonathan are a prime example of this type of relationship. "After David had finished talking with Saul, Jonathan became one in spirit with David, and he loved him as himself" (1 Samuel 18:1 NIV). The Lord helped create this bond between David and Jonathan. He put the two together for covering and protection.

The Lord loves us through our lifetime friends, our besties. We make a commitment to each other. We stay loyal, becoming a safe haven for each other and so much more. Days or months may go by without us speaking or hanging out. But when we get back in touch, we pick up where we left off, feeling like we haven't missed a beat. The tears, the ugly cry—we've seen it without the filters. There is depth to this relationship. Friendship can be risky because we become vulnerable, and friends have expectations, but in lifetime relationships, taking the risk often only increases the bond. These kinds of friends are considered family and may become closer to us than some family members.

Several places in the book of Proverbs give wisdom concerning good, solid, lifetime friendships. These proverbs are about friends who provide feedback and truths that liberate us to become our best selves. We help each other define our characters and are honest—but careful—in our conversations. Real friends stay close when times are tough (Proverbs 18:24). Good friendships are good for the heart and soul (Proverbs 27:9). Solid friends are there to love you at all times and in spite of yourself (Proverbs 17:17).

Good friends also love us by sharpening us through correction, like when we might be getting in our own way. I remember one of my close friends telling me I tended to cut people off and not let others finish their sentences. At first, I was offended. I responded from a place that lacked understanding. I often overthink things people say, but I let her comment simmer a bit. It then made total sense. While it bothered her that I was talking over her, she also checked me for the betterment of my people skills. If my goal is to be like Christ, then me being considerate of others is also a part of my goal. Now I write things down while someone is speaking, I wait for them to finish, and then respond. I try to be as selfless as possible in my relationships.

Advisors or mentors are another group God brings into our lives (which can include family and friends) to help us through certain situations or choices. These individuals can be spiritual or financial advisors, and possibly life coaches. They can be a short-term connection that helps you through a specific time in your life. The person who offers wise advice can already be in your life, like a spiritual mother or father, your parents, aunts, uncles, or a person you lean on. Whoever they are, this person gives sound counsel and may offer prayer for a difficult or complex situation. What makes this person an advisor or mentor? You trust them enough to bring a situation you are dealing with to the table. They sit down with you, bringing their expertise and thoughts, as well as ideas you have not considered. It's wise to heed their counsel and be open to their authority, which comes from a more knowledgeable space.

I've worn both hats: mentor and mentee. These relationships can be fun and liberating as we are getting answers, or rewarding and strengthening as we help someone else get answers. And both roles work to fulfill our purpose.

Ways to fulfill this role of mentee are by showing gratitude for the mentor's time and commitment to us. Age doesn't necessarily define the qualification of a mentor or a mentee. As a believer, I've had to learn that it's okay to be held accountable and to be careful not to fall into the trap of a know-it-all—disdaining counselors or advisors because I have more years or feel I've experienced more in that space. Are there moments we may not agree with counselors? Yes. There is a way to respectfully disagree. Mentees may even sharpen mentors through the way they interact or by bringing up a new approach they recently learned and then introduce to the mentor. But the key to a good mentee-mentor relationship is that the mentor can and does guide and use their wisdom to help you grow or overcome what you are facing.

This relationship can even turn into mutual friendship over time, but it may be one-sided for the assigned mentor because they are the one bearing the weight of counseling and supporting another person. This isn't wrong or unfair, as the mentor understands the assignment, is anointed to pour, and is equipped to fulfill. And it's important you are clear on the assignment if you become a mentor. I learned the difficulty of mentorship when I was called to mentor people going though a very rough time in their lives and didn't fully prepare myself for what it would take. While they wanted me to be their equal/friend, I lacked clarity of the Holy Spirit's guidance concerning this relationship. As a result, I was hurt after the assignment was fulfilled. To fulfill your purpose as a mentor, you need to maintain enough distance in that relationship to give the proper wisdom, as well as open yourself to others' emotions and take on that weight as you offer knowledge. Relying on the Spirit is sometimes the only way to get through and grow in your own ways.

The Holy Spirit helps us compartmentalize relationships, define who's who in our lives, and what to give in each relationship. Just because a close friend or relative committed to be with you for life, that doesn't mean they are the best person to listen to for wisdom concerning every matter in your life. The Holy Spirit will show us the people, why they are there (short- or long-term), and how they are to be listened to (deeply or casually). He will show you "who's who."

Prayer

Father, help me know who's who! I thank you for calling me to love others and their differences; anoint me with the patience to be kind and considerate of any growth spurts those around me may be going through. I thank you for strengthening me to give others the same grace I'll need at times. Forgive me for any toxic behaviors I've held on to and guide me to become the best I can in my relationships. Remind me that being a Christian means I should test the influences around me against your Word. Help me see anything in others that doesn't align with you, and allow me to sense any unseen forces working to trip me up. Help me test situations with your unction and direction. Remind me to assess myself as well. Help me test others' conduct using the gift of discernment. As John 7:24 reminds me, "Do not judge by appearances, but judge with right judgment." I ask for your help as I assess where each person should be placed in my life. Help me see the purpose of every relationship—how I can serve them, and how they can also support me as I move forward. Help me know who's a mentor, a mentee, a colleague, a friend, an associate, or just a momentary connection. Show me how to communicate effectively so that my words reach their soul. I ask that you connect me with genuine people. Remove jealousy, manipulation, or deception from me and those I spend time with. Surround me with strong people— strong in the mind and spirit. Thank you! In Jesus's name, amen.

Chapter 16

Sound Check

> *Iron sharpens iron, and one man sharpens another.*
>
> **PROVERBS 27:17**

In a sound check, an engineer makes sure the sound is right. They give you onstage monitors that are close by so you can hear and feel yourself. There are also speakers on the stage that feed to "the house"—the audience—to make sure the crowd hears all the instrumentation of your performance. They push you to make sure you sound right. But there are some engineers who don't work in your best interest. They'll give you a hard time when sound checking just to make it look like they're in charge, when the goal should be to make it easy for you to give your best and sound good when it's time to perform. Or they don't put in the effort at all.

Who does your sound checks with you? Is your "engineer's" ear listening to you and at the same time listening to the Holy Spirit? Do they have your best interests in mind, correcting what needs to be corrected? I remember chatting with my mother about books I was reading on apologetics. A lot of the books I picked up were also borderline outside of my belief system. I'll never forget when my mother said, "Girrrrl, you're reading something you shouldn't be reading. That ain't it! This ain't adding up!"

God has also given me a husband who is an excellent sound check manager. I remember riding in the car with him—still mad at him about something he'd already gotten over. I have a tendency to hold on to things, which is something he's been helping me to assess so I can move forward. This is where the fruit of the Spirit perseverance comes in. (That's another conversation. Ha!) Well, in this instance, one of his favorite songs came on, and he yelled with his hand in the air and fingers snapping, "Ayyyyye." I abruptly turned off the radio. He yelled, while also laughing, "You're a hater, bro! Get over it!" This tickled me so much, I couldn't stay mad. I began laughing because he called me "bro" and that slip of the tongue totally embarrassed him. He turned the radio back on and maintained his good mood. I'll admit, I wasn't in the right spirit. I was definitely killing the vibe with my bad attitude. But what I appreciated was that my husband knew exactly how to roll with me, and gently set me right. He operated in the right spirit. He knew how to co-exist with me and adjust the frequency.

We need these kinds of engineers around, like my mother and husband. They ensure we are on the right track. During that time in my life when I was studying books contrary to biblical truths, I called myself searching. I wanted to be too grown for my own good. Too grown to see some truths with my own eyes. I needed the eyes and ears of others to do a sound check.

God told Adam and Eve to not eat of the tree. They ate anyway because they wanted to "know." Some things, we don't have to "know." And as a result of their choice, they couldn't walk in complete freedom, as God wanted, because they had eaten of the tree that gave them harmful knowledge. Some fruits are forbidden.

Unfortunately, we turn our attention to forbidden, off-limit things. I remember wanting to be so knowledgeable and so creative in order to seem brilliant. I entered a gray area that was very ambiguous and left me with a lot of questions as a result. I needed the correction to put me back on track. The same type of correction is necessary when we hold on to harmful behaviors that are off-limits. We need someone who can tell us how we sound, and then help us correct it so we perform the way we're meant to.

Yes, some people can be dangerous and attack us to bring us down, but the good engineer (or listener) will listen from the heart. Their spirit will move them to correct what doesn't match our purpose. Look to the people you've already identified as soul sisters, advisors, forever friends, and people gifted with wisdom. They'll push you in the right ways and help you refine your spirit.

When God asked Cain in Genesis 4:9, "Where is your brother, Abel?" it's recorded that he replied with, "Am I my brother's keeper?" But the answer is yes. We are our brother's and sister's keeper, and we have the same kind of keepers watching over us. God shows us how to be a keeper and to love one another. So don't think it strange that he's showing someone else how to love you. With love comes correction.

Father, I am forever grateful that you sent me family and friends who are in alignment with you. Please help me remember that you are a God of unity and community. Help me to see and discern the people you have assigned to my life. Show me the right people who will be great engineers in my life: sound techs who will tell me when my sound is off, when my spirit isn't right, when I am not making good decisions, and when I'm not on the right frequency. Sound engineers who I can enjoy life with, and live the principles of the Kingdom, while not feeling like "too much." Thank you for the truth that you're allowing me to experience. I'm sure that it'll set me free. Thank you for the good sound and beautiful aroma you've called me to put out. Thank you for loving me through the people I can call a village. I ask that you strengthen me to discern wisely and to not operate as a "know-it-all" when they are there to give me answers. Mature me to know when it's my time to pour and to listen. Grow me up, Father! In Jesus's name, amen.

Life Engineers

> *Speak the truth to one another.*
>
> ZECHARIAH 8:16

The idea of having an engineer fine-tuning your life sounds modern, but the concept is far from new. And one of the best examples that shows how much we all need sound checks and an honest engineer in life is David and Nathan.

King David had a close relationship with God, so much so he's called a man after God's own heart and one of the first examples a lot of people think of when they think of a God-fearing biblical hero. He even wrote tons of psalms that help us learn how to communicate with God and check ourselves. But when David saw Bathsheba bathing on her roof while her husband was off fighting in David's army, it's like all his internal spiritual monitors went dark. He only heard what he wanted to, not the Spirit's warnings. And after David listened to his desires and committed adultery with Bathsheba, his spiritual dissonance only got worse. When Bathsheba told David, "I am pregnant," David proceeded to handle the situation almost as if he'd forgotten what God's voice sounded like at all. He tried to manipulate Bathsheba's husband, Uriah, into sleeping with his wife. That way, Bathsheba could claim, "This is my husband's baby," setting David free from responsibility and "fixing" the situation he'd helped cause. But that plan fell through when Uriah decided to obey his military orders and oaths. So, desperate, David issued orders that led to Uriah being killed in battle and then took Bathsheba as his wife.

David thought his cover-up worked. But his engineer, the prophet Nathan, had his ear tuned to the Holy Spirit and the lesson God was sending. Nathan did a sound check and told David, "You're off! You've walked into another man's house, a good, honest, loyal man, and taken his wife." As a result, David saw the error of his ways and repented. And for the rest of his life, he worked to regain his connection with God.

So again, I'd like to evaluate with you. Are your engineers making sure that your vibe is correct when you step out on stage in front of an audience? Are they considerate of your assignment on the earth? Or are they hesitant about telling you the truth? Do they have the right motives concerning you?

While your good friends and loved ones are being a sounding board for you, will you get mad if you hear the adjustment? Will you get offended if they turn your mic down? Will you think they're trying to cut you off? Or will you trust they're adjusting for your own good? As a professional singer, when I'm at a venue and my sound check time is up, the engineer may shut my mic off. It can be frustrating if I don't feel like I'm ready to perform, but sometimes if my time is up before I'm ready, that could mean I spent my time talking back instead of focusing on preparation. Sound checks are so necessary.

But be careful. Who is checking your sound? Have you prayed about your "Nathan"? Who's listening to the Holy Spirit with you? Sometimes our messengers change according to the seasons of our lives. Stay before the Lord, asking for them to be sensitive to his leading and the wisdom they speak into your life.

Chapter 17

Perfect Harmony

> *I therefore, a prisoner for the Lord, urge you to walk in a manner worthy of the calling to which you have been called, with all humility and gentleness, with patience, bearing with one another in love, eager to maintain the unity of the Spirit in the bond of peace.*
>
> **EPHESIANS 4:1-3**

I remember being the kind of church member who would leave an event because of the unaddressed issues and personality differences I had with some other member. I grew irritated with the unfiltered questions some would ask me, or the statements folks would make "in the name of Jesus." Earlier, we talked about how the Lord dealt with me and showed me how easily I cut people off rather than learning how to work with them. But this experience taught me something deeper about myself—that I wasn't taking the time to work in harmony with those around me. One time, I even heard God tell me, "Don't leave too soon this time."

Don't get me wrong, there are moments when the Holy Spirit will have you get out to avoid mess, harm, or worse. However, in this case, the Holy Spirit convicted me and had me see I was also throwing off the vibe with others, contributing to a dissonance in the air that was driving us apart. It was made clear I was good at text messaging, but I was not the best at verbal communication. So I learned to verbally communicate my thoughts in a way that was understood, and to dwell and work among the brethren without making the room uneasy because of my disposition. As we all got on the same wavelength and began to understand where the other was coming from so we could adjust our tones, things worked much smoother. The Holy Spirit got me together by showing me the beauty in togetherness.

It's also a fact that one sound alone never sounds as rich as many working in harmony. I saw an example of this in my music-writing process. I used to try to write songs all on my own. While there may be some who are skilled and gifted with the ability to work by themselves, God left room in me to need someone else. I *can* do it alone, but I feel I deliver my best songs with help. Soon, I began sharing my ideas and being patient with the process because I could see the rewards.

When writing songs with some folks, depending on the situation, I could either feel inadequate and mentally compare myself to the other writers in the room and get frustrated and shut things down, or I could figure out how to collaborate so we came out with the best possible product. When I first started writing with others, if I didn't have words right then to put in a verse, I'd back away or write down my ideas privately. If I was really stuck, I'd usually say, "Let's go on to the next song," and that would be my way of quitting. However, one of my friends I wrote with said, "Let's just let the process do the work." This stuck with me. Sometimes the process could be just sitting there—just "being" is still a way of finding harmony. We were in sync. If someone new came in during one of our "being" times and didn't understand our process—it may have knocked us off course. But if that person observed, they came to understand the nonverbal communication and what was happening in the room.

This type of harmony is sort of like a friend who gives you eye contact, and without having said a word, you start to laugh. The eye contact is your language, and when it's used you understand, you are in sync. There are joys to these moments when our souls and minds are knitted with someone else's. It can be liberating and encouraging to know that we aren't alone. But to get to that place, it takes work and commitment. We can't abandon the process or think our opinions, feelings, and thoughts are more important than those we're collaborating on life with.

The Holy Spirit is the one who brings us together and holds us there, guiding us toward the circumstances needed for harmony to take place. It is his desire to fellowship with, and dwell with, God's children. Then he dispenses affection, compassion, understanding, and love among believers for us to be together, help one another, and raise each other up.

Before Jesus left the earth, he specifically prayed for the body of Christ to be unified as the Father, Son, and Holy Spirit are unified. Each person of the Trinity has their distinct roles and personalities, but they are in complete harmony—there's never conflict or strife. The apostle Paul understood these words and said Christians are to be united in spirit (Philippians 2:2). This means to have one driving, compelling desire—to build up God's kingdom. A goal of having God's will fulfilled and bringing him glory.

How? Paul's letter to the Philippians laid out a plan. "Do nothing from selfish ambition or conceit, but in humility count others more significant than yourselves. Let each of you look not only to his own interests, but also to the interests of others" (Philippians 2:3–4). What Paul is getting at here is finding a balance, a harmony, in how we see others compared to ourselves. If we act out of self-ambition and only look out for number one—what is going to arrogantly promote us, and us alone—that puts us at war, in strife with everyone else. The arguments and fighting begin. It's flesh work at its best, because usually to make yourself look good you have to destroy another person. Nothing is accomplished other than a mess. But when you work from humility, you see the needs of the other person first and have more understanding and patience—with others *and* yourself as time goes on.

Your heart is the only one you can honestly examine. This kind of introspection keeps us from quickly putting ourselves on the top and working to keep the other person underneath. So the next time you're in a situation where it feels like things are out of balance and you to want to run or lash out to avoid the personal discomfort, take a moment to listen to others and see if you can match their vibe and create a wonderful harmony together.

Prayer

Father, I thank you for teaching me not to leave too soon. Continue to develop in me the desire for unity. I ask that you forgive me for returning bad energy. Sometimes I misunderstand people, but I ask that you not allow me to operate from a place of revenge but from a place of harmony. Help me learn to manage different personality types so I am not creating any forms of awkwardness, as you're a God of peace and unity. Help me bring life to the party. Help me not leave before it's time, and see the beauty in connectivity and balance. Allow me to be so in sync with you that I became a master of personality skills. Assist me in understanding others so I see deeper into psychological differences and act in kind. As you grow me in harmony, please help me enjoy togetherness and not forsake assembly with others. Thank you for the joys of learning with others. Purify my heart so that I may see your work and ways you're telling me to go while dealing with others. In Jesus's name I pray, amen.

Chapter 18

Say It with Honey

> *Let no corrupting talk come out of your mouths, but only such as is good for building up, as fits the occasion, that it may give grace to those who hear.*
>
> **EPHESIANS 4:29**

The Holy Spirit gives us guidance on how to communicate with one another. Some people are "full of it" (and I'm not talking about God's Spirit). But the Holy Spirit will even guide you on that. Stop ignoring it! The Holy Spirit gives us nudges and memos. He tells us how far to go. He really does. If you were to assess your entire life, how many times can you say the Lord was giving you small warning signs, flags, pinches, or reaching out in another way?

One thing that those nudges remind us to do is watch our

tone. Even if the Spirit doesn't pat you on the shoulder each time you need the reminder, God has given us Scripture to make the message clear: Don't forget to say it with honey! Say it like you'd want it said to you. Until we get a taste of our own medicine and hear how we sound, we're not as enticing or cute as we think! Ever had something said to you that didn't feel good? While we should be mature enough to receive the truth from wherever it comes, it can become a bitter task when it's not given with some consideration or a bit of love.

When we make sure to consider what's behind our words, people might say we go the extra mile when we give a little more backstory or care. Some with blunter styles may think it doesn't take all of that. However, when you care it shows, and others feel it. And erring on the side of caring and carefulness is better than pounding someone with your words, whether you mean to or not. The world may reward big mouths and overconfidence, but that's not God's way. Going back to his wisdom in the Bible, "It is better to be slow-tempered than famous; it is better to have self-control than to control an army" (Proverbs 16:32 TLB).

Ever deal with someone who's so quick with you? Like when you're going through the checkout at a store or dealing with someone in customer service—they're quick with you and have no desire to make you feel welcomed. It's just, "What do you need so I can be on to the next?" The Lord works on our patience and helps us to be slow tempered. God isn't impressed with social media numbers or how well we market ourselves and gain followers through our public persona. He's most concerned with how we manage the invisible parts of ourselves—everything that has to do with the soul.

I remember doing tasks for my parents when I was younger

and they'd say things like, "Don't be quick with me." Or my husband telling me, "I'm not a business transaction" and to "slow down" when I tried to treat him short. My husband and I sat down and read Scriptures on love, and he made me realize Scripture states that love is not irritable. This checked me real quick. Even with how we handle things using God as our center, we tend to operate from an irritable place when things get busy. I also understand learning this lesson can take time and persistence. A few years prior, my parents told me to increase my patience levels. I researched the meaning of *irritable* and found it means "to be easily annoyed" according to Dictionary.com. If we are to love everyone, then we should be willing to give ten extra words to make the next person feel welcome. That may be the little bit of honey needed.

Obscene words, filthiness, foolishness, bitterness, lying, backbiting, or anything like that should not be found in the mouth of Christians. Faithfulness, sincerity, pleasantness, gentleness, and truth should empower the believers' words. And these words or expressions are meant to be delivered to one another in a low, humble tone and be uplifting. If you can't communicate in this way, be quiet.

Add salt to your words. And I don't mean saltiness! When used properly, salt takes a bland piece of meat or a vegetable and adds flavor, making it more agreeable to your taste buds. Salt also makes things pure, helping to preserve the good and keep out the bad. Salt is considered a healer. We need to live according to Ephesians 4:29: say only what is good and helpful to those you are talking to, and what will give them a blessing.

That doesn't mean every conversation has to include the name of Jesus. In fact, sometimes it's just not appropriate when someone goes on and on with a spiritual conversation and it's neither the time nor the place. But God's children are centered on being Christlike, listening to the Holy Spirit, letting him guide how we answer each person and handle each situation we encounter.

Have you ever spoken before thinking? Or had something come out of your mouth and thought, "Where did that come from?" Or you said something and regretted it later? The Holy Spirit can help us get control of that mouth. Jesus said when dealing with the Pharisees trying to take him down in the moment, "Out of the abundance of the heart the mouth speaks" (Matthew 12:34). In other words, what you let fill your heart will control your mind. He continues to talk about what flows from these lips: "I tell you, on the day of judgment people will give account for every careless word they speak, for by your words you will be justified, and by your words you will be condemned" (verses 36–37). That should be enough right there to make us drop to our knees and ask the Holy Spirit to transform our hearts, so what comes out of our mouths is pleasing to the Lord.

Another person who had a lot to say about our words was King Solomon in the book of Proverbs. One of my favorite verses he wrote on the topic is Proverbs 15:4: "Gentle words are a tree of life; a deceitful tongue crushes the spirit" (NLT). A healthy tree grows; you can seek shade, refreshment, and shelter. A fruit tree offers food, sustenance for those who eat it. Positive words can offer the same as a healthy tree. But the fruits are not just for those who are friends and in agreement. The tree also provides for the enemy and opponent, giving them something good that can nourish in positive ways.

Of course, words go both ways. The end touches on a deceitful tongue, meaning it's crooked, twisted, or warped. Something very unhealthy and out of order. Someone can be moving forward in life and then a person says something that is out of order and disturbing. It breaks the person down, breaks their spirit. And where a tree grows slowly, needing time to reach a place it continues to nourish others, inappropriate words can do severe and immediate damage, tearing down and prohibiting growth in the people affected.

Here are some warnings and some encouragements when it comes to our conversations:

- Be attentive, watch your "careless" or "useless" words. I remember saying things like, "I'm going to keep it one hundred." This was once my excuse for a lack of salt or honey to my speech. Sometimes when there is an issue to be addressed, I will take a pause, maybe even for a day or two, then address it head on to ensure I am responding from a place of love rather than a place of emotion, rage, or anything outside of the Spirit. I had to learn the way of truth so that it is easily digested. Sometimes the truth isn't what we want to hear; sometimes it can be a bit more digestible because of how it's given.

- Take care of your body. Being sleep-deprived, overworked, overwhelmed, tired, distracted, or even hungry can cause you to flip out and say unnecessary things. Don't engage in a serious conversation (or if you can, just be silent) if you realize these negative things are a part of your life in the moment.

- Be careful about what you let into your inner self. Once something enters, it affects your words and actions, and the root cause can be very hard to remove.

- When someone hurts you, express your thoughts and feelings to someone wise and safe. Holding things inside and pretending, "Oh, I'm not angry," or saying, "What you said hurt me, but I'm okay" is not good. If you can't talk to the offending person or don't feel it's wise to discuss anything just yet, wait. Talk with a trusted relative or friend. Pray with them about your next steps in dealing with the difficult person or situation. Journaling or creating an art piece or song might be a good option as well if that's how you process things. Get your stuff out on the table but not by telling someone off.

- Ask the Holy Spirit to give you the ability to forgive. If you need an example of what forgiveness looks like, check out Jesus's parable of the unforgiving servant (Matthew 19:21–35). Keep in mind that forgiveness is between you and the Father. But reconciliation is possible only when both parties admit their wrong and want to do better by each other. Do not keep subjecting yourself to a toxic person or situation if neither is going to change.

Scripture tells us that our glory has to do with our ability to overlook an insult, and that also goes for not delivering an insult in the first place. I know some of us may be reading this saying, "Well, shoot, I've got a long way to go." Our ability to ignore ignorance and work toward bettering our soul is accredited to us as God's children. It's like an exam. How many exams have we failed because we are anxious to show someone they can never disrespect us?! Everything should be done with honey.

Prayer

Father, I thank you for your grace and mercy. You've allowed me to learn and see how I can be better with my words. I thank you for the power you've given me through my tongue. While understanding you've given me a superpower that is connected with your kingdom, I ask you to organize my thoughts and help me be gentle with my speech and think twice before delivering words that could damage someone. Father, I understand my speech will have a lot to do with my future, and some doors you'll allow me to walk through. Please hold my tongue before I say too much. Halt my speech to call me into line. I'd rather lack a response for a moment than damage someone for the long haul. If this isn't truly in my heart already, please put it there. I understand the issues from my heart will flow through my speech. Please cleanse me from anything that does not match your heart. If I am called to deal with an issue, please rationalize with me. Let your Holy Spirit guide me on what makes sense by your approval. Thank you for the new flavor to my speech. I accept your work for me. In Jesus's name, amen.

Chapter 19

Girls' Night Out

> How good and pleasant it is when
> God's people live together in unity!
>
> **PSALM 133:1** NIV

The other day, while out for a girls' night, I mentioned to the group of friends at the table that they were the people who made me come alive.

I laugh louder, I laugh harder, I think more.

I never leave my girlfriends feeling the need to evaluate what I say and doubting whether or not I was safe in saying what I said. With this group, I trust that everything I leave on the table is safe. Any secrets I've shared with them aren't a threat to me.

Not only are they great and solid friends, they're solid people. I call them sisters, and I don't use this term casually. When I call them my sisters, I mean that what we say is true in heart and in deed. It's not just a figure of speech. We also understand that sisterhood doesn't mean sameness, but it also doesn't mean separation.

My friends and I argue or disagree about things at times, but when one is wrong and needs to grow, we admit our wrong to each other, pushing pride aside and "not canceling each other" but encouraging each other instead. It doesn't matter how angry we have become with each other—we're committed to staying friends.

I've grown to understand the power of togetherness. Because of the past friendship and relationship issues I've discussed, I preferred to be by myself. But I got to a place where I asked myself, *How can I expect to stay in heaven, where there will be a community around me, if I don't know how to enjoy being around people now?* Yes, I get it! Many people are shady and there is such a thing as boundaries. And there are personal boundaries that definitely should never be crossed. But sometimes you don't know how much you've boxed yourself in with self-made, artificial boundaries until you find the people you click with, and trust comes into the picture. Having a connection that is freeing, with people who will support you and know you well, opens you to knowing and experiencing life in the way it was designed to be lived. After all, God created us for close relationships and community, starting with the first humans he made.

Sadly, out of fear many people do break all ties with people who could benefit them. Actually, they even do it to God because in their eyes, one side of the relationship isn't working to their benefit anymore. When this happens, it shows that person doesn't understand a key ingredient to healthy relationships—being long-suffering. This was my challenge. If you showed your colors once, even if it was because of a down moment, I showed hardly any mercy because I didn't want to get hurt again. A friend once asked me, "Have you ever had to say sorry?" or "Have you ever hurt someone?" Living in fear is not how life should be. Now that I've learned friendships come with hurt as well as tremendous joy, I find many answers to my life questions while talking with those in my circle.

I can't stand bad vibes and tension. But I love being with friends who notice if one of us is the cause of it so we call it out, we admit to it, apologize for it, and work on it going forward. Friendship and people are beautiful. Whoever isn't meant to be in your life, learn that and adjust as a healthy, growing adult, but also watch to see who is sent to be in your circle. The right friends will help you be a better person, mirror Jesus, think better, manage money better, and so on.

That's not to say friendships only mean good times and benefits; close connections are also meant for the low times in life, and are even more important then. Have fun together, yes, but also discover creative ways to encourage one another and motivate each other toward acts of compassion, doing beautiful works as expressions of love. There's a verse in Hebrews that comes to mind, which was written while the early Church was facing death and persecution: "Let us think of ways to motivate one another to acts of love and good works. And let us not neglect our meeting together, as some people do, but encourage one another, especially now that the day of his return is drawing near" (Hebrews 10:24–25 NLT).

Hebrews encouraged the believers then, and I hope it encourages you now. Staying together and meeting regularly—whatever you're facing, this will help. A night out with my girlfriends strengthens the connection and good vibes—whether we're celebrating or consoling someone—and it can do the same for you if you open yourself to the blessings.

Prayer

Father, I thank you for my growth and maturity in this season. I thank you for helping develop me into a woman who is pursuing kingdom living. Righteous living. And life lived in your community of people. I declare over my life that I am a kingdom citizen, and I am unapologetically living by kingdom principles. I ask that you continue to allow me to examine every space that I go to and connect with the people who will benefit my life, and that I benefit theirs. Show me the balance of boundaries and love. In Jesus's name, amen.

Chapter 20

I Hear Voices

> I pray that your love will overflow more and more, and that you will keep on growing in knowledge and understanding. For I want you to understand what really matters, so that you may live pure and blameless lives until the day of Christ's return. May you always be filled with the fruit of your salvation—the righteous character produced in your life by Jesus Christ— for this will bring much glory and praise to God.
>
> **PHILIPPIANS 1:9-11 NLT**

Think of voices you recognize even when you don't actually see that person. After listing those names, evaluate your relationships with them. How many years have you invested in that relationship?

I get joy from just hearing my husband's voice, walking to the door after a long day of work. (When we first started dating, the deep, manly texture of his voice made me fall in love. I began looking forward to calling just to hear him say anything to me. When he says "Yo!" to get my attention, for some reason it makes me melt.) I know my mother's voice when she's in another room. Sometimes I'll call my mother's phone and hear, "Guten Tag, ich heiße, sprechen Sie Englisch?" It's my father, speaking in German, pretending he's someone else. I usually say, "Dad, quit playin." We'll laugh it off because in that moment, his cover is blown! I know my father's voice!

My brother does this obnoxious laugh when something is really funny to him. It tickles me because it feels like home. I enjoy knowing when he truly finds joy or a moment of laughter. When my father calls my full name, "Kierra," I know I'm in trouble. If he calls me "KiKi" or "Keek," I know things are not so bad. In even how those voices call our names—and who calls them—we have an idea of what may be coming. My brother would yell and say, "Go and do such and such." I wouldn't move. But when my mother yelled, I'd jump up with a bit more enthusiasm, that voice an authority in my life. This is my family; I've spent time with them my whole life. I know their voices, their laughter, when they are pleased with me, and when I'm in trouble.

The more time we spend in the Word of God and in prayer, the more we are going to become familiar with the Holy Spirit's voice as well. He becomes "family." More time in God's presence helps me to know if he's pleased with the things I'm doing. Also, as I learn how to recognize the Holy Spirit's voice, I can be confident in the decisions I'm making, knowing he's leading and guiding me. It's essential to learn the Holy Spirit's voice and follow instructions.

Can you say you recognize the Holy Spirit's voice the same way you know the voices of family? How much time do you give the Lord? Is his voice becoming more familiar to you as you've spent more time thinking about him?

Let's look at how we can better hear and understand that voice—the tone and meaning behind the words. The ability to know who and what voice is speaking to you is called discernment. According to Merriam-Webster, discernment means "the quality of being able to grasp and comprehend what is obscure; an act of perceiving something; a power to see what is not evident to the average mind." The definition also stresses accuracy, as in "the ability to see the truth." Spiritual discernment is the ability to tell the difference between truth and error. It is basic to having wisdom.

Usually, if you hear or sense voices in the absence of any physical source, it may cause some people to think, "This person is strange." Or some question, "Are they hallucinating, or mentally ill?" Now, I will say if you're having experiences you know aren't sitting well with your spirit, then you should see a mental health professional. I am a strong advocate of mental health maintenance. (It's not something to play with.) But when that voice comes from the Spirit, the experience is different: soothing, connected to our heart, in the form of a strong voice in our head or even an actual voice calling to us. It guides us toward beneficial things, not things looking to harm us or lead us to confusion. It aligns with the Bible's teachings. (And if you are ever questioning if the voice is the Spirit's, please reach out to someone you trust and/or your pastor to help you assess!)

Someone in my life who knew the Holy Spirit's voice especially well was my aunt Janet, and I relied on her when I was young. As a teenager, and into my young adult years, I totally focused on the question, "Who is my husband, Lord?" Every year, my aunt Janet came to visit from Monroe, Louisiana. Aunt Janet had the spiritual gift of prophecy and I looked forward to her visits. She often pulled me to the side concerning my question, saying, "No, this is not the one." I don't know how many times I heard Aunt Janet repeat this statement. I began to depend on her like a guide. At one point, though, Aunt Janet got silent on me. Instead of telling me details about a young man, or saying something pertaining to my life, she said, "You already know." She began to teach me how to discern, how to listen to the Holy Spirit for myself.

Now mind you, my father is a pastor and has been my pastor my entire life. From childhood on up, I listened to his sermons. His messages included guidance and instructions I specifically needed to hear. The Holy Spirit spoke through him directly to me. But I closed my father out for a short time because he was, well, Dad. Unfortunately, I made decisions I knew the Holy Spirit was not leading. Half of the reason I messed up so much in the past—I didn't listen! I refused to recognize the important voices I needed to hear. Though for a very short period of time I thought my parents couldn't relate much, or were trippin', I soon learned that they were actually some of my best friends and greatest guides. It didn't take me long to realize the value of their voices, because after making a poor choice, my mind or heart was often redirected to the initial advice they had given me.

And they gave me a lot of good advice when it came to

making good judgments. I grew up hearing my parents often say, "Something ain't sitting right." I'd bring a friend home from school for my parents to meet, then hear, "Something ain't sitting right." They'd be talking about a matter concerning our family, or a situation at the church: "Something ain't sitting right." They would turn the matter or the person over and over again in their minds, mulling it over, praying about what was in front of them, but also seeing deeply, with a spiritual eye. Seeing what I couldn't see on the surface. My aunt Janet and my parents attempted to teach me how to discern. They wanted me to learn how to listen for the voice of the Holy Spirit for myself.

If you don't have an Aunt Janet or person in your life to learn from, the story of the prophet Samuel hearing God for the first time is a great example of learning discernment. If you're not familiar, Samuel learned to hear and discern the voice of God when he was very young. The first time God spoke to him, he thought it was Eli, the priest who helped care for him. God's voice came to Samuel one night, and he kept running to Eli saying, "Here I am; you called me." Finally, Eli realized God was attempting to give a message to Samuel. Eli told him, "Go and lie down, and if he calls you, say, 'Speak, LORD, for your servant is listening'" (1 Samuel 3:1–14 NIV).

And when it comes to discernment, don't underestimate or minimize the direction/warnings from the Holy Spirit as only your "intuition." It's often God still walking with us, even when we're resisting walking with him. It's not just "something" that told you. It was God! Imagine how life could be if we were more committed!

So learn to listen for his voice. Go back into silence. Wait. Listen again. Say yes. Be ready to obey.

Prayer

Father, I thank you for trusting me with your voice. I thank you for allowing me to communicate with you so I can do well in life. You want what's best for me! That is exciting to know. Knowing you've sent people you speak through is even more liberating. Sometimes this spiritual walk can feel intangible, or complicated, while sifting through my emotions to know your voice. However, as well as I can tell a loved one by their voice, I declare I know yours. You are my loved one. You are the ultimate One. You are my God, I am your child. So remove any hidden thoughts that keep me from being in touch with you. Assure me in the Spirit that you haven't abandoned me, and you never will. Today I acknowledge you as Lord of my life. Settle my emotions so that I'm self-aware but also spiritually aware, and in tune with you. Make your voice clear to me. As I'm excited to talk with others, I'm even more excited to hear from you. Keep talking, Lord! I'm listening! You are the living God and you speak. In Jesus's name, amen.

Chapter 21

The Vibe of Your Music: What Is It Making You Do?

Then Jesus said to him, "Be gone, Satan! For it is written, 'You shall worship the Lord your God and him only shall you serve.'"

MATTHEW 4:10

I remember driving with my mother around the time I had just gotten my license, and I had one of my favorite rappers on. I turned the volume up, and my mom said, "Turn the music down, so you can hear what you're thinking."

I said, "Mom, it's okay."

Then she added, "And you're going too fast. There's a spirit in the music. It's making your foot too heavy. That's your problem." I did tend to drive too fast and had been getting speeding tickets left and right. She finally hit the power button with a bit of authority and said, "While I'm in the car, the spirits we choose to ride with will be at my discretion. Slow down and get us there safely."

I wasn't really listening at the time and I didn't understand it then, but I totally get it now. As I play this back in my mind, I see myself and Mommy as if it's a scene in a movie. I was going 80 in a 65 zone, but because of the vibe I had around me and the tone I set—that what I was doing was cool and made me grown—I moved with the wave of the vibe I set. What the vibe made me feel made me be okay with a speed that was illegal.

Mommy went on to explain how the adversary works and that music is one of his leading avenues. The Bible makes it clear that Satan was one of the most beautiful and powerful beings ever created. Lucifer stood out as a supreme archangel, surpassing heavyweights like Gabriel and Michael. No red suits, pitchforks, or horns for this guy—he was, and probably still is, drop-dead gorgeous. He also may have been one of the first worship leaders.

The Bible shows us in several places that angels are gifted with musical ability (for starters, think of Jesus's birth or the worship songs angels lead in Revelation)—and Job 38 tells us, "Where were you when I laid the foundation of the earth? Tell me, if you have understanding. . . . when the morning stars sang together and all the sons of God shouted for joy?" (verses 4 and 7). What we translate today as *morning stars* clearly refers in the original language to the angels there when God created the world. And Satan—one of the top angels before he rebelled—would have been a part of this amazing heavenly choir.

But whether or not Satan was in charge of music before he fell from glory is probably of little consequence. The real takeaway is *why* he fell—pride. The reason I tend to think of Satan as a former worship leader is the powerful connection that exists between music and pride. You have the ability to influence people's emotions through your gift, getting your words stuck in their head. I can't imagine many other skills that would make a created being so full of himself as to think he could overthrow God himself.

I'm not saying that any music artists are the devil, but as an artist, I've had to be conscious of what I put in others' minds and their atmosphere. When I consider many of the songs I've played in my casual time, and how well I retained the lyrics, I realize what I've rehearsed in my mind and allowed in my space. And while there are many, many singers who keep their standards and make a positive impression on the mainstream market, I'm sure you can name some musicians whose behaviors and modes of operating shift as they become more focused on fame, often leading to songs that are less enriching when it comes to the lyrics.

It's important we don't accept an underlying negative or harmful message that is released through the music we listen to. For example, I remember the feeling I used to get when listening to one of my favorite R&B artists. I'd yell out, "This is my soooong." And would begin wanting to be around the guy I was dating at the time. Until I began cutting those types of songs out of my life, I didn't realize that some of the music I listened to was leading me toward temptation. When you're desperate enough to be delivered, you'll be more than willing to remove anything attached to what had you bound, broken, or confused.

Vibes don't just come in senses we get or people who approach us. They can sneak in and affect us for good or ill through what we willingly allow into our lives. The music we listen to can lead us into times of praise and worship, and connecting with the Lord, or it can lead us into the enemy's further destruction. Be careful.

Prayer

I understand there are laws in your kingdom. So if any negative spirit is driving me, remove it now! Father, I enjoy different genres of music, but allow me to identify and pinpoint the sounds that call up any forms of darkness. I ask for your gift to discern if there are songs I'm playing that are taking me away from you and toward the devil. Today, I choose to be selective with the vibes I introduce myself to through conversations, alone time, music, or even the books I read. No matter how good the beat is, or how popular the song, please help me to be responsible enough to choose life. Now that I am aware of the spiritual connection with music, I ask that you help me not make any excuses for my favorite influencers. Cleanse my ear gates and mental lobes. The ways I've unintentionally taken on from the vibes I've lived with, I release and lay at your feet. Thank you for growing and developing me to be driven by your Spirit. Help me remember too that some of my favorite people don't live with the same standards or spiritual agreements. Since I don't know what others believe, help me to be careful with my choices, and follow your guidance, when it comes to what I permit to enter into the spiritual gates of my innermost being when with other people. Today, I'll make better choices, and will gladly choose sounds that agree with heaven. Thank you for helping me through this. In Jesus's name, amen.

Don't Be Stupid

Do not be conformed to this world, but be transformed by the renewal of your mind, that by testing you may discern what is the will of God, what is good and acceptable and perfect.

ROMANS 2:12

Because we are in the world and have sin in our lives, our ways of processing day-to-day decisions and why we do the things we do aren't always guided by the right motives. Which is why we may want to listen to a certain type of music, spend all our money on certain entertainments, focus on things that benefit us more than others, or delight in things like hot gossip. But as we've explored in this book, that is no excuse for behaving stupidly when it comes to our spiritual and earthly lives.

Whether it's translated as *foolish, unwise, thoughtless,* or *careless,* "stupid" in the Bible refers to someone who does not accept God's rule. Their inner perspective is lacking, they are not listening to the Spirit of wisdom to regulate their behavior. *Foolish* may be a gentler way of putting it, but the implications are the same. It's acting without thinking of the consequences, being unable to see the overall picture, having spiritual blindness, and being unreasonable, ignorant, shortsighted, mindless, and rash. A stupid person is being inconsiderate of themselves and those in contact with them.

In the Old Testament, "stupidity" is used in reference to being brutish like cattle. It also refers to those who worship idols (Jeremiah 10:8; 10:14; 51:17). Idolatry back then, and today, means to give oneself to an object, another person, or a damaging emotion, instead of looking to the True and Living God. It's putting one's trust solely in a job, marriage, relationship, money, children, or any such thing as your rescue and help.

Wisdom, on the other hand, is appropriately applying one's knowledge and experience. The Holy Spirit freely offers wisdom to those who ask. "Wisdom cries aloud in the street, in the markets she raises her voice; at the head of the noisy streets she cries out; at the entrance of the city gates she speaks: 'How long, O simple ones, will you love being simple?'" (Proverbs 1:20–22).

It's a gift from God. "If any of you lacks wisdom, let him ask God, who gives generously to all without reproach, and it will be given him" (James 1:5).

One receives wisdom by humbly realizing it's needed in our lives. Those who walk in wisdom do not claim to be a "know-it-all" but look to the Father for his direction and decision making. Those who follow Christ are constantly praying for spiritual or divine wisdom and understanding.

Chapter 22

Spiritual Junk Food

> *Test everything; hold fast what is good.*
> **1 THESSALONIANS 5:21**

When our hearts and minds are full of junk, it's harder to discern what the Holy Spirit is saying or not saying. When we are feeding our spirits with the right material, Scripture reading, and prayer, the Spirit is able to live comfortably within us. He's able to sift and notify us when a thought is or is not from God.

When the Covid pandemic first started, many people of all ages became homebound. For many, screens became their best friend. Their television, computers, tablets, and cell phones became the place to turn when bored. (You can probably relate!) Many fun TikTok challenges were created to bring us closer with loved ones. In addition, necessary conversations started to happen, and we got rest from the day-to-day rush. For me, once I saw how refreshing a bike ride, cooking at home, and time spent with family could be, my values began to change and I noticed how much attention I'd started giving things in life that were truly good for me. I even noticed I had more time to pray. My parents hosted prayer calls to keep us connected, and this is when my prayer life grew.

Sadly, I also realized how little I'd prayed before the pandemic. There was so much the Holy Spirit was trying to get to me back then, but because I was so busy, I lost sight of so much. Also, a steady diet of corrupt programming was part of my daily routine. Violent or sensual movies. Series filled with manipulation, deception, and lies. Plenty of garbage on social media.

I know about creating good eating habits. I remember when I lost ninety pounds; I was so excited about reaching the weight goal, but I discovered the work I had to do wasn't just about dropping sizes. There were long-term, internal changes and goals I still had to reach. I saw how removing the carbs and sugars drastically improved my weight loss, but I was more focused on losing the weight than interested in, or even thinking of, healthy eating needing to become a permanent lifestyle. I was just happy I had achieved a good weight goal because now I could shop for what I wanted to wear.

Later, I started to gain the weight back, but this time I gained it with comfort and age. I looked back and realized I'd felt better when I cut out the carbs and sugar, but at this point in my life I opted to cut them because losing them was good not just for my body but for my heart and how I wanted to function in the world. I just wanted to enjoy going out, and I soon lost sight of my body type and my ideas behind what it needed to be. I had to do what was good for me as far as eating and living my life even if no weight fell off.

I had to come to grips with another shift of change as well. One of the truths was that before I focused on simply giving my body what it needs, I kept snacking, thinking smaller portions meant better, and not getting meals with great nutritional value. I'd grab and go when my body didn't need the quick hit of chips, it needed the platter of veggies. It needed the supply of energy and antioxidants to ward off sickness and to fulfill purpose. When I dove into this space of wellness, I also learned that this too was an act of worship. Science says that even the foods we eat contribute to our mental state.

Just like eating much of the wrong kind of foods results in health problems, turning toward the wrong spiritual or mental nutrition can destroy the parts of you that need to be healthy in order to function as you were designed by God as a whole. An example of this is my husband when he's into a game he's playing. He's very passionate about the game, and like many of us when we want to win, he tends to yell or show disappointment. However, Jordan and I have discovered that his interactions with that game may have trickled into his communication with his wife. Not that I'm innocent; I work so much, and he and I have noticed that I sometimes treat him like a transaction or business deal when I've been taking too many poor "nutritional supplements" in my life.

Sometimes passions like work or entertainment can become junk not because they're *bad*, but because of how much we consume or how we misuse them. Deep down, we know that. You may have even rolled your eyes a little when you read it. But that doesn't stop the truth, that a steady diet of earthly things results in an ear and mind that are not sensitive to the Holy Spirit. When we are also taking in Scripture and prayer, the Spirit is then able to live comfortably with us to sift and notify us when a thought isn't from him.

The Bible is spiritual food. God's Word provides:

- Milk for the new believer who is just starting to grow (1 Peter 2:2).
- Meat for the mature Christian who is asking for more spiritual insight and understanding (1 Corinthians 3:2–3)
- Bread, daily sustenance spiritually, physically, mentally, and emotionally (Deuteronomy 8:3; Job 23:12).
- Things sweeter than honey, pleasure and delight of our souls (Psalm 119:103).

The Scriptures are more than something to casually eat, like a snack on the run. Several places in the Bible emphasize the importance of sitting down, enjoying the meal, chewing the food, not just gobbling it. And then letting your food digest as you meditate and reflect (Psalm 1:1–3).

So leave the junk food in your life for special treats; find time for the nourishment you need in your life.

Prayer

Father, help me remember that my body is yours. First Corinthians 6:19–20 tells me my body is a temple to house the Holy Spirit. Forgive me for overcrowding you, Holy Spirit. I ask that you give me the discipline to choose wisely what I fuel my mind, body, and spirit with. Please forgive me for selfishly giving so much time to things that don't always connect me with you. I've studied the ways of the world through social media more than I have studied your words. Help me put more edifying material in my real-life timeline so that even in my spare time, I find you. I know that even some of the music I listen to may be contrary to what you desire for me, so please help to find fulfillment in new and progressive ways of entertainment. Today, I give my body and ways to you. Cleanse me of the junk food and replace it with whole foods. Thank you for your patience with me. In Jesus's name, amen.

Chapter 23

No Discounts

> *So do not throw away your confidence; it will*
> *be richly rewarded. You need to persevere so*
> *that when you have done the will of God,*
> *you will receive what he has promised.*
>
> **HEBREWS 10:35-36** NIV

Louis Vuitton doesn't go on discount. So why should you? Don't settle for less. With the Holy Spirit, you have a whole lot to offer.

Sometimes in society, women are made to feel they shouldn't take pride in themselves or speak up, and when they do, it can be seen as "too much" in certain situations. But God didn't design us with timid spirits and tamed-back purposes. (If you want a whole book that looks at why God didn't design women to sit back and be quiet, check out my first book, *Big, Bold, and Beautiful.*) But how many of us have dealt with manipulation, or toxic relationships, longer than we should have, in ways that have harmed us and our paths? I can count on one hand how many situations I've tolerated. I often felt guilty for allowing things to go further than they should have. Have you gone through similar things? I've evaluated what I've done as a person, a friend, a sister, a girlfriend, etc., and considered if the others involved matched my efforts. Sometimes seeing the differences in effort can cause us to reassess and see if we've sold ourselves short.

That's why it's good to have someone around who will tell you, "Girl, you're shortchanging yourself." The Spirit does the same thing in us—the last thing he wants is for us to think and act like we're less than we're worth. I know sometimes we don't believe in ourselves because of past mistakes, or we simply are not seeing the beauty that God sees. However, the Lord wants us to know everything he's made is expensive and of great value. Just think; he thinks so highly of you, you were worth dying for. And he put a personal coach inside you so you can be reminded of your value every day.

So how do you handle yourself, knowing this? I'm not saying walk around being entitled, arrogant, or rude, but do not let yourself be abused, mismanaged, or taken advantage of in any way. If you're uncomfortable with something, you have a right to express yourself; if you don't set boundaries for yourself, others will set them for you. Has your tolerance level for certain things increased because you've always had yourself on the clearance rack? What have you allowed that you know the Lord wouldn't be okay with? Take a moment to assess and look deeper into your life and how you've managed yourself with others. You're worth everything in God's eyes—but if you give away parts of you like your joy, your peace, and your self-worth, it starts to affect your life, relationships, future, and everything else. Leaving you feeling like the exchange rate is shortchanging you, so you have nothing left for yourself or anything of value to offer—when the opposite is true.

There are many examples in the Bible of people the world discounted and God used to do amazing things, but one I especially like is Ruth. Her book of the Bible is one of the greatest love stories in the Bible, and a lot of times what we focus on in that story is how Ruth was willing to leave her homeland for Naomi and how Boaz had to go out of his way to marry Ruth and redeem her family. But what I like to focus on is what the story says about Ruth herself, and why Boaz was so attracted to Ruth when she arrived. We see with Ruth and Boaz, there was an equal exchange. The relational value was there. One reason for that relational value is that, from the start, the Ruth who arrived in Israel was determined to be true to herself—this was a woman who gave up a safe future (staying in a land she knew and letting her parents find her another husband) because something inside told her to go even after being told it was a bad idea. And she was confident, even though she had little reason to feel that way when she arrived. As a widow, she wasn't seen as having a lot of value in that society. As a foreigner, she was worth even less to the people around her. But even though she was poor and ridiculed, she never doubted herself. She knew the value she had in God's eyes. And while Ruth was out working in the field to support her family, just doing her thing, this man was attracted to her work ethic and the way she carried herself. What that tells me is, when you understand who you are and whose you are and find security in that, you attract the things you're meant to find and grow as a person. You attract purposeful relationships built off true, inner value that allows you to flourish in your life. Whereas when you're off course and see yourself as less-than and not as deserving, you build relationships out of vulnerability or insecurity and stay stuck in an old path.

Ruth also chose a mentor to follow, who helped her find a task that allowed her to show people who she was, and who helped her make the connections she needed. When you follow the right mentor/advisor/counselor as a guide to help and encourage you, especially one who is tuned into the Spirit, you find yourself in the right place mentally and empowered to do what's needed.

Ruth stayed focused through the poverty and judgment of others because of the interior and exterior guides she leaned on. When you discover your talent and remember your purpose, your focus isn't competing with anyone else or letting people define you. You become so focused that you never even notice what others are doing. You simply walk in what you are called to do, and the greatness God has planned finds you. You then don't become the goal chaser or the money chaser. It all comes to you. The dream chases you. This is the Holy Spirit working for you. There is a confidence the Holy Spirit wants us to walk in so that we deliver at our best. He wants you to live life to the fullest. He wants you to win. He wants you to live according to your value. We are predestined. Hence, there's a part of our makeup that is necessary for the success of something. Because of your abilities, the dream needs you to act in order to succeed. Because of your mind, the dream needs you to focus and persevere in order to succeed.

Again, I'm not saying become arrogant, but to become confident in how the *Lord* has created you and what the *Lord* has given you and called you to do, and not focus on what a person, relationship, or job is saying you're supposed to do, or focus on anything that is limiting what you *can* do or who you are.

Your relationship with the Holy Spirit adds higher value to you. You are beyond designer label. The Lord will nudge you when you're asking for too much, or when to ask for more, but he will never tell you to settle for less. He has a way of guiding us with humility that empowers us in new ways. The Holy Spirit doesn't only give us the capability, he also gives the character to sustain you as you walk through the doors he's opening. We mess up at times, but he gives us the pinch to get back on course.

It's okay to be shy if that's your nature—Ruth herself seems pretty shy at times—but it's not okay for it to overtake you or become an excuse, causing you to discount yourself. I had to learn the right time to break out of my shell, and that time happens when you remind yourself of the VALUE you bring to the table. We sometimes need to remove ourselves from situations that don't match our values. With the God of the universe and Creator of all as your friend, you have a lot to offer. Period. While you're in the field, you're mastering the skill. In this process, you're becoming confident but being clothed with humility.

Prayer

Father, thank you for trusting me with the gifts you've given me. I am thankful you've given me the opportunity to experience your goodness. Everything that is attached to me is by your doing. Thank you. Father, I have shortchanged myself and it has exhausted me. Today, I want you completely involved in every relationship and choice I make. I don't want to mismanage what you've given me, as I know it is a way to show you my appreciation. So, please mature me and guide me to live an enriched life of wisdom and perseverance. I declare that you're helping me see deeper and hear deeper while in conversations and interactions with people around me. Thank you for allowing me to know what to give and what not to give. Thank you for allowing me to be vibe-sensitive, to see how to move as the seasons change. Most of all, I thank you that you're allowing me to see me through your eyes so that I am no longer thinking less of myself. Thank you for believing in me enough to bestow blessings upon me. Thank you for helping me see all of the beautiful parts of me, and the ways that make me different. Thank you for tailor-making me and stitching me together better than any designer could ever do. The way you've made me connects me with purposeful relationships and solutions I didn't know were mine. Amen.

Proximity Vibe

> *Do not be deceived: "Bad company*
> *ruins good morals."*
>
> **1 CORINTHIANS 15:33**

A lot of times, it's easy to tell where people have been or figure out what they've been doing based on the scents they carry. For example, if you spend a day at the beach, you'll probably smell like sand, water, and fresh air. Or if you've been smoking or hanging around people who do, the pungent odor makes it hard to deny even with a powerful coverup spray.

Being in close proximity to certain people can be similar—we take on the vibes of the individuals we spend time with. And just like a physical smell, those around us can pick up on the spiritual essence we carry with us and determine the type of good or bad company we keep and person we are becoming as a result.

Think about what vibe you give out. Who are you in proximity with on a daily basis?

Do you spend most of your time around people who are thinking, talking, and acting unwisely? If so, expect to start thinking, talking, and acting like a person who is not intelligent and is prone to foolishness. Been around evil people? Expect inner malice to start flowing from your lips. Been around angry, short-tempered people? Expect to start spouting off.

As Proverbs 13:20 tells us, "Whoever walks with the wise becomes wise, but the companion of fools will suffer harm."

That's because when you're around something so much, you become desensitized to it. While we all know this truth deep down, when it's actually happening we often need the reminder to help us reevaluate. Just like cigarette smokers can no longer smell themselves after umpteen years of smoking because they've become so familiar with the stench, if you hang around with unwise, foolish, angry, hostile, and negative people all the time, pretty soon you don't even realize how much they've seeped into you and dulled your spiritual senses. The condition of the heart can become hardened. You are no longer yielding to the Master's touch.

But in the same way, if we spend time in the Father's presence, in his Word, listening to his voice, hanging around believers who love Jesus, we become more like him. Jesus had a distinct way he talked, walked, and prayed, as well as how he loved the people around him. And the people who stayed near to him often were changed from the inside because of the lessons they picked up through simple proximity. Are you walking in close proximity with Jesus, spending time with the Master? How does that affect what comes out of your mouth? How you lead? How you love others?

In Hebrews 12, the writer calls believers to get in close proximity to the Savior. To "fix" one's eyes. If your eyes are staring intently at Jesus, you've got to be close to him. He's definitely in the room. And it means we are not looking at him with a quick glance or an "Oh, yeah, I see him" while we are half watching. This is a stare down, an on-purpose, intense observation. What's the result of this kind of serious observation? He begins to rub off on us. We smell like him—a sweet, pleasant aroma from being in his presence. And as we spend time with the Lord, more of his reflection should also shine through us.

What are you looking like? Smelling like? Depositing into this world? Those around you will know who you've been hanging out with—and odds are, you'll notice the difference as well.

And God is also moving closer to you to help you find that proximity vibe. In fact, the entire Trinity is working together to create a close bond: the Father is hovering over us, the Son is walking each day with us, and the Holy Spirit dwells inside us. Each one is near us daily, moment by moment, closer than our next breath. As we are in closer contact with them, they peel away our sinful nature.

If it helps, you can think of the process like an onion. Each layer of the onion is like a layer we put between us and God. And a lot like peeling an onion, removing those layers can be painful for us, but when the divine God team of the Trinity is alongside us, they're helping remove the pungent layers so that with time, the tears this process causes become less and less. The Trinity's goal is for us to reflect and resemble Jesus Christ, to become holy. And as the layers are removed and we get closer to the core—closer to our inner, truer self—we're set apart and ready for God's work in the world.

In order for this to happen, time needs to be spent in proximity to God's Word, God's Spirit, God's people so we take on the vibes and good qualities and leave behind the old, smelly version.

Prayer

Father, thank you for showing me the depth of the company I keep. Please surround me with people who will complement the glory you've placed in, and on, my life. Allow me to do the same for others. I'm sorry for smothering your majesty and wonderful Spirit with spiritual acquaintances that might not have made you feel welcome and pushed you away. Today, I ask that you clear my circle of any sinful cycles, behaviors, and attitudes. If I'm too close to darkness that is leading to more compromise, or comfort with things I shouldn't be around, please help me to release any hindrances or influences. Thank you for the confidence to be spiritually selective concerning what I let in my proximity and spaces. Thank you for purging and consecrating me. Thank you for helping me learn the difference between being alone versus loneliness. Today, I declare I'm no longer making connections out of vulnerability but from a place of security. You're growing me and helping me value everyone but also helping me manage my space wisely. I'll continue to consult with you concerning nearness in time, space, and relationships. In Jesus's name I pray, and declare. Amen.

Chapter 25

I Washed a Stranger's Feet

> *When pride comes, then comes disgrace,*
> *but with the humble is wisdom.*
>
> **PROVERBS 11:2**

So often, we can think of ourselves too highly. That's because it's easy to focus on our own point of view and needs, and what we want to do, since we know exactly what we want and frankly want to get it. Personal gratification is hard to give up! Plus, it's hard to put ourselves in someone else's shoes or do things that seem to place them "higher" than us.

Jesus shared a moment when he washed the disciples' feet. When he was finished, he mentioned he expected us to do the same—to not see ourselves as better and treat others as equals—and to accept those he'd send and minister to them. Unfortunately, when we deal with certain people, accomplishments can often go to our heads and we forget to be friends, servants, and sisters because we've been so busy mastering being bosses, queens, and leaders. I've often had to be sure I don't drive myself to a place of always seeking to share knowledge or self-help on social media because I'm feeling my own wisdom, to the point I forget how to apply the wisdom I've gained from the Lord.

Many times, I've displayed a level of pride through competition. In those moments, because I didn't acknowledge it as competition or blatantly did things that harmed other people, I gave myself grace concerning this when I shouldn't have. But the truth is, competition and pride were in my heart, and they compromised the integrity of my intentions. The Boss Babe era and my drive for entrepreneurship reinforced this behavior until the Lord convicted me and I began seeing that the people I kept around me were a network I'd created to advance myself versus being pure friendships that supported me. All of us were connected by what we could get from each other, and our interactions were based on personal accomplishment and how we could build ourselves up, versus helping and valuing one another. As a result, behaviors I thought were building me up were instead holding me back, keeping me from becoming someone who could truly lead and mentor. I was forced to evaluate which people could help me grow and operate on a higher level and cut away the rest.

My pride and need to be first also came through in how I communicated. I mentioned earlier a friend telling me, "You should learn to stop cutting people off when they're speaking." I told her I didn't mean any harm, but just because I didn't mean harm, that doesn't mean that it's an excusable way of life. While I was still learning how to correct this habit, I began prefacing any interruption with, "I don't mean to cut you off, but . . ." and continuing with what I had to say—until I did this with my father. Before I could get my comments in, he said, "Your preface doesn't excuse your pride. Allow me to continue and hold your thought, please." This hit me like a ton of bricks because it was truly a different perspective, and he saw deeper into me than just poor communication skills. It challenged me to learn the essence and patience of listening to hear the next person instead of only seeking to be heard, and that I really did have to learn to write out what I wanted to say and wait to say it.

If I had the same posture and disposition as Jesus, these times in my life would have gone so much differently. Jesus even calls himself a teacher and a master, but he still bent down and washed another's feet.

How humble are we? Do we really think of our neighbor as higher than ourselves?

The Holy Spirit has been working with me when I'm out with others to not make the conversation about me. To show I'm interested in what they have to say. To be selfless. To think of them as more noble than me. For you, it might be something like being kinder to new people in your circle or learning to pay more attention to what people may need for support and be afraid to straight-out ask for.

It helps us grow in humility if we thank God often, recognizing he is in control. Focusing on giving thanks also puts a stop on pride because the Lord becomes the center of our focus—not us. Confession of one's sins and wrongs reminds us that we don't have it all together. It also helps to laugh. Yes, laugh. Learn to laugh at yourself and not take life so seriously. Be a listener. Take an interest in the other person's story, and don't dominate the conversation and make it all about you (and when you do, catch yourself and take the extra humble step of apologizing. Shout out to all my extroverted sisters out there!). And finally, put others' needs before your own. This is the way Jesus lived every day of his life, and so many lives were affected by his approach, even when he came in contact with someone for just a moment. Jesus now lives in us through the Holy Spirit. Which means we can tap into that power and do likewise.

Prayer

Father, help me to see when pride is sneaking inI know I've had arrogant and selfish ways that haven't allowed me to consider the other person, and sometimes I didn't notice those ways in the moment but only after the harm was done. Please help me so that pride doesn't become a part of me or ruin my relationships. I understand that admitting to and seeing this about myself takes a lot of effort. It won't feel good, but out of it will come good. Help me to be securely clothed with humility. Today, I acknowledge that my neighbor holds greatness, and I'm anxious to wash their feet by way of service, love, and forgiveness. I declare you are even greater! Father, in my walk with you, help me be bold about my choices, but please also help me not separate myself from others. I declare you're cleaning up all parts of me. I acknowledge your sovereign role in everything! In Jesus's name I pray, amen!

Chapter 26

The Dating Pool

> *Keep your heart with all vigilance, for*
> *from it flow the springs of life.*
>
> **PROVERBS 4:23**

Maybe you've heard the phrase "the dating pool" before. The *pool* part refers to the overall group of single people available to you to date—but the problem is, the number of people in the pool at one time is often very large, making it really hard to narrow down which people you should interact with. And a lot like a swimming pool full of people, you may wade into some unexpected surprises if you're not careful. The water might be dirty and not good for you to swim in at the moment, so you need to hold off before jumping in. The chemicals in it can sting your eyes over time, and if you ignore the sensation, it spreads until it's hard for you to see who you're hanging with or how to find your way around. And sometimes you want to do laps because everyone else is when you should really be chilling in the shallow end, getting used to the water until you understand how you're meant to swim (and so you don't unnecessarily hurt yourself). God has given us the ability to sense the things we'll encounter in the dating pool—like when we're ready to date someone, when we should back away because the relationship could hurt us, and when we simply need to proceed carefully—but we need to be open to the Spirit's guidance when we get the nudges.

The nudges and vibes we feel when dating are a powerful thing. Before I surrendered to the Lord, I wasted a lot of time on guys because I hoped things would work out or change down the line. Once I surrendered to the Lord and became clear in my purpose as a woman of God, I knew what I wanted in life, and I allowed myself to be single and not always jumping into the next big relationship. Once I got out of the pool for a little bit and could better assess the waters and the people in it (and how I should spend my time in the pool when I entered it), I knew what I wanted in a partner and could better sense if things would work out. Some guys I dated were just a good flirting time for a moment I could paddle away from, while with others I needed more time to assess the situation and see if our life purposes were matching up so we could swim at the same pace together. This is when I realized I didn't have to say yes to the first good thing just because it seemed close enough. My mother always told me, "Don't just say yes to anybody," and as I got into Scripture, I saw God was giving the same advice about waiting for the right relationship. (Check out Proverbs 3:5–6, Romans 12:1–2, and 1 Corinthians 13.)

It once annoyed me how much my father was in my head about some guys he didn't feel great about, until I began understanding the Scriptures and wisdom of the voices of good counsel in our lives. When I was younger, I wasn't thinking about everything that should've been considered for marriage. If I had married the first few people I thought were good for marriage, I'm not sure we would have made it a week. I for sure would have been unequally yoked if I had ignored the vibes I felt when it came to maintaining honesty, finances, spirituality, etc. I knew there was more at hand to deal with than the surface challenges we faced in those relationships. That's how the enemy works—he is a master at distracting and prohibiting us from seeing the big picture, clouding our vision when he can. God's way is always and has always been for us to be clear, and he sends us those nudges to help keep us off the paths we choose for earthly and physical reasons and steers us toward the paths that will lead us to a relationship that will spiritually and mentally fulfill us. As a result, things I began noting from Bible studies and lessons those around me shared in choosing a mate pointed me to a realization that marriage is a God thing and that there's more than romantic love involved.

I had to stop lying around and stop being dedicated to ghosts. I can hear you wondering, "What do you mean *ghosts*, Ki?" Men who would disappear, not return my calls, or do anything that would make me feel like they weren't there. In other words, stop committing to people who aren't committed to you.

Other things I discovered that were important in relationships were spiritual unity and life-purpose compatibility. For the relationship to work, your purposes must match Ephesians 2:10: "For we are his workmanship, created in Christ Jesus for good works, which God prepared beforehand, that we should walk in them." You can't have a solid relationship or get married not knowing your purpose in life. The person you plan to marry must have similar purposes. That way, you can support each other as you grow together, and no one is holding someone back to benefit themselves. That also taps into the "equally yoked" idea in the Bible; it has to do with sharing the same faith, definitely, but it also has to do with being able to support one another and move forward as one.

Another thing I learned is that there's no such thing as a perfect person. If you're out looking for that soulmate you see on TV and in the movies, you're going to be pretty disappointed and lonely. You're going to have fights, and you're going to have moments where something they do drives you crazy—and you drive them crazy. You can't cut off a relationship because of little things. But the big things do matter and can be signs to watch for. Which is why emotional intelligence is also part of building a good, healthy relationship. Can they handle their frustrations and talk through what they're feeling? Are they willing to share their hard times? Can you do the same with them? Godly partnerships are built on having good communication and respect. If a guy is prone to outbursts and childishness, it is often a warning sign they aren't ready for something serious with you. Avoid any signs of anger, addiction, bitterness, and selfishness. They're signs of insecurity and brokenness that you're in no place to fix.

I was often drawn to the "bad boy" when I was dating. Trust me, the pain isn't worth it. And when you are in a good place yourself, the bad boy probably won't seem as attractive because you're focusing your heart on the traits that matter instead of the ones that seem appealing. Don't let yourself get used to dysfunction so it's all you want to live in. Don't let a hurting part of yourself choose what is good for all of you. When we choose from a broken place, we only choose a little better than what we had last time. So it's just as important to focus on your emotional intelligence and get yourself right as it is to look for someone who will treat you right and be the good guy you want to have in your life.

The thing is, God won't tell you who to date or who to marry; he may give you signs he approves it, but he won't tell you who. He may give you the vision or traits that they must have, but not directly point out who it is. You need to lean on what your heart—your Spirit-led heart, not the Hollywood-flavored romantic version—is showing you. Remember: generous men show kindness and prosper; a good relationship is based on partnership; love is based on trust, trust is based on truth, and an emotionally healthy person tells the truth.

Prayer

Father, thank you for your grace. Please cleanse me from any ideologies of this world and culture that may not be in alignment with your will. Forgive me for accepting relationship models from the world as a normalcy for me. Today, I give you my life again. Thank you for the space to rededicate my life to you. While dating, please discipline me to choose from a place of knowing exactly where I am and where I'm headed. You're a God who is already in my tomorrow. Please help me consider the future and how our purposes must match. Show me how to have fun while dating but keep me clean and pure. Help me to know when to get out of a situation before it becomes an entanglement.

Help me to lay aside fleshly desire and dig deep to see what you're saying. I'll need you to accompany me on this journey, in this life. Remove the weight of loneliness so I'm choosing from a whole place and not one of perceived emptiness. Thank you for your protection. Thank you for counselors and advisors who will help me to consider things I may be overlooking. Open my heart to them so that I can listen well. In Jesus's name I pray, amen.

Chapter 27

All Over the Place

> *I will instruct you and teach you*
> *in the way you should go.*
>
> **PSALM 32:8**

I remember I had a guest over and I couldn't find my keys. I put down my shoes and everything I was carrying to look for the keys, and they were right on the counter. The Lord had me scout the room and see how messy it was. I was embarrassed because my clothes were everywhere. Shoes were in hampers with clothes, girdles were on the counter, and many more things were in places they shouldn't have been. There was no organization. I then accepted the gentle note after seeing my way of organization: I needed to settle down and clear out some things.

This reminds me of a time I was praying for a few things in my life and I kept asking the Lord, "When is it supposed to happen?" or "Am I supposed to be attached to a person, or a project?" During that time I had been ignoring the Holy Spirit. When we do that, it can clutter up our lives so we can't find the things that are important, even if they're right in front of us. It can push us into confusion or into a dull heart.

In different translations, the Bible describes the hearts of the people as "heavy and fat" (Matthew 13:15). When I read this, it sounds unhealthy. It is alarming. Usually, fat around the heart can lead to inflammation and other major health complications. If I were to go to a doctor and they showed me fat around my heart on an X-ray, I would be motivated to eat and live differently.

What if we were able to see what was happening in the Spirit with our hearts using a spiritual X-ray? Some of us have the gift of visions and intercession, and so have a glimpse of what this might be like. However, for most of us I wonder, do we downplay the spiritual because it is the unseen? We don't see it among all the "clutter" of the world. When I thought more about that, it convicted me to understand the detriment of being away from the Lord's will so it is made real. It also heightened my senses and desire to know that my spiritual health can slip through the cracks if I let it. It's all on me. God doesn't force us to do anything. Loving him is a choice. Doing his will is a choice.

In what ways have I grown to be toxic with myself and the Holy Spirit? I began getting used to pointing the finger at someone else until my father called me out, and his voice started ringing in my head: "What did you do?" There comes a point where what is happening is not about anyone else. Reflect with me. What choices have we made to put space between us and the

Holy Spirit? What have we digested continually that we haven't intentionally gotten rid of after we've realized it was there?

Like my father's words to me, having someone who can help us see these spots in our lives is important. Which is why churchgoing is necessary. Hearing the Word from our pastors is necessary. But after we leave church or hear someone's advice, what do we do with the instruction? If we don't take it in and start clearing out the junk, it's like going to the doctor and getting a prescription for a medication to keep our hearts clear of the fat, and we never take it. We end up in a worse condition, one that could have been avoided.

The goal is to stand clear and to be healthy. To be well and to do well. To be abundantly blessed. The beauty about spiritual health, and walking with the Lord, is that it overflows and infiltrates all parts of our lives when we aren't half steppin'. When we go all in, we see the fruits and truths manifest in our mental health, financial health, relational health, and more.

We also have to go all in on listening. I've had to learn to stop ignoring what I'm feeling. It's like ignoring the Holy Spirit. If we sing songs like "Holy Spirit, you are welcome in" but ignore his attendance, then how does he feel? Would you want to stay if I ignored your nudges? If I keep calling someone's name, and they don't hear or don't listen to me or they don't turn around and look in my direction, I'm going to ask if they can hear me. If I try it again and they don't respond, I usually walk away.

If we're all made in the Father's image, then more than likely there are some things we do alike. Remember, what you practice becomes a habit, and it's easier to ignore something or stay on the same course than take the difficult step of making a change/new habit. I'm afraid I once upon a time made a habit of ignoring the signs. If I had known that I was in a sensitive space of learning the Holy Spirit's voice and guidance, I would have paid attention to my apprehension.

Apprehension, reservations, or questions should always stand as a flag to let you know there is more to consider. Sometimes the afterthoughts should be considered—we're human, so there are things we miss the first time that we need to think more about—but learning the afterthoughts that are sent to us to consider by the Holy Spirit versus "the after attack" of doubts and misleading thoughts makes a difference. With the Holy Spirit come answers, understanding, and interpretation that improve your life. Even when it hurts. The after attack, however, feels like condemnation (Romans 8:1).

Another way to view how the Spirit sends us signals to change is seeing them as warning signs along the road. Signs are usually posted on the road to let you know what's ahead. For instance, there's usually a sign to let you know you've reached a dead end or where you need to take a detour to get back to where you need to be. The Lord is so interested in you having answers that he finds ways to get them to you. Or look at how we've progressed in technology; now on our maps, in our phones, it shows where there's traffic, an estimated time of arrival, the speed limit, and other suggested routes. This is how the Holy Spirit works!

I remember being on a flight—in fact, it's one I briefly mentioned in an earlier chapter. The flight was only supposed to be an hour, but it turned into three hours. The pilot came over the intercom to inform us that there was too much traffic to land. There was also weather ahead that we needed to avoid in order to land safely. Sometimes we think God is being difficult when really he's saying, "There's too much traffic for you to land." This could mean, "People will be in the way, but I need you to have this time for yourself." It could mean, "This is not the storm for you to weather." If we trust God and believe he's always a thousand steps ahead of us, then we won't rush to do things on our own.

I have most definitely ignored a ton of the warning signs. What have you had in front of you? Sometimes it's so easy for us to reflect on what has happened, and not consider what is happening. And just like my house, the clutter in our lives can pile up without us being fully aware of how bad it's really gotten, to the point it's immediately evident to others and messing with our day to day. But nothing comes out of nowhere and signs are all over the place. We just have to focus on the one who can help us clear through, clean up, and get things back on the right track in our lives.

Prayer

Lord, we've been connecting for a while, and you know my imagination, my schedule, my funds, and everything else can be all over the place. Today, I ask that you still my soul and spirit, and I declare order in my life. Father, when I'm all over the place, I find I'm vulnerable and anyone can move me, so I ask that you come into my heart and still the troubled waters of my soul. I thank you for slowing me down so I move at your pace instead of my frazzled speed, and I trust that your timing is perfect. I bring before you my habits, asking you to become the center of my life. Help me see the signs you send that show me truths about myself. Cleanse me. Just like I need to keep my belongings organized, remind me that my choices, thoughts, and motives have to remain in order. Help me practice mindfulness. I've committed to remain focused on you. I also see that the winning part of the equation for the life I want to lead is to return, rest, get quiet, and trust you. I accept your place in my life. In Jesus's name, amen.

Chapter 28

People Change

Above all, keep loving one another earnestly,
since love covers a multitude of sins.

1 PETER 4:8

Some people change for the good or the bad, and it can be for a lifetime or for a season. We have the same ups and downs as we grow and mature. Since we have inconsistencies within ourselves, and our spiritual walk, then it's only fair to give grace to others, and continue to until we can fully discern where their path leads.

Do we always have the right vibe? No. Do we aim to have a heart of repentance and a praying spirit? Probably! The same is true for those around you, and that has to be considered as you interact with friends, acquaintances, and even the person down the street you sometimes see getting their mail. Unless you live with a person and are glued to them at the hip, you really don't know what their prayer life is like. (And even then, you still won't really know.) You don't understand the struggles they're facing or the doubts that might be creeping in or the confusion they're having in the moment. Just as you war in your mind from time to time, it is very possible for someone to take on a spirit of anger, envy, jealousy, bitterness, deceit, etc. And it's possible for us to misinterpret it as well, even react in a way that causes more harm.

In the dark, forces are always at work, seeing who they can keep with them in their misery. Misery loves company, and that's not true just for friends who gossip all day. Misery loves company also applies to the dark principalities. They don't like to be alone. If we understand that, then we'll remember that the adversary is always on the prowl. Interestingly, not everyone will be as vigilant as you may be, with the same awareness of what happens in the spiritual world. We have to make a conscious decision to always discern the spaces we are in and help those close to us navigate when we see them slipping. The Lord is often speaking and giving us guidance in this area.

Sometimes it's hard to let go of our frustrations and worries with other people because of our fear of what they'll do with it. However, we never have to worry about releasing too much with God. If we allow him, the Holy Spirit will work alongside us to free us from what we've shared while also helping us learn from those shifts and changes and give us clarity in the relationships.

Another thing I've realized is that sometimes the issues we struggle with when it comes to those around us is not so much about the other person changing than our changing and no longer wanting to deal with ways of living or choices that we once tolerated during a more unseasoned time in our lives. Growth is change. So as we grow in understanding, lessons the Spirit reveals hit differently with each new revelation along the journey. We begin to see motives and truth when it comes to friends and acquaintances, as well as the truth and changes within ourselves. Have you ever said things like, "I wouldn't have handled that like that"? I have. Now think about things you did in the past; are there times you would say the same to the you of years or even months ago? Your reasoning or perspective might've made sense before. However, when you review it again and reconsider some of your then-logic, it's like a different person was making those choices.

We can't fault each other for change. It's part of being human. The beauty in walking with the Lord, however, is he's constant. God doesn't change. The same goes for the things he reveals to us through the Spirit to wake us up and get us on track as we grow closer to him and who he wants us to be. God always shows us signs for a reason, even if we don't want to see them as his messages and guidance every time. The Lord has convicted me about this. He's said, "That was there all along. You just got comfortable!" And like we extend grace to ourselves when we have these revelations, we need to do the same with others. Our awareness and location in our walk with God may be in different places at different times.

When we take the time to really listen to the Word of God and connect with his Spirit inside us, we have a better chance of considering where people are in relation to him and his will, as well as how we are meant to interact. In fact, the Father led me to a godly perspective that helped me navigate and manage relationships with a better understanding. It is that relationships are like clothing textures. Some fabrics are too thin or thick for the season we're in, and other pieces don't have enough elasticity for what we need to do, leaving us uncomfortable and ill-fitted for the occasion. And even with some clothing that has elasticity, when you wear that piece too much, it loses its form, which changes your love for it and its usefulness in your life. Some textures are super cozy but don't fit the situation we are in, and some may not have the strength needed to sustain storms we face. All the textures have a place, and we wear them accordingly and see the differences between each but value them all.

I've had to learn to not see change as a negative thing because many changes in my life have been for the better. And even those that have come from damage or simply poor choices, I'm grateful because they helped me grow into who I am—and I'm grateful for those who stuck with me and helped me navigate the change.

Prayer

Father, thank you for individuality. Thank you for giving us all a different makeup that adds value to this world. Mature me so I'm able to recognize differences and can accept others' growth. Thank you too for allowing me to see that changes in others are not all about me, and remind me of this truth when I start to assess others from that perspective. Just as you have a plan for my life, you have a plan for others' lives, so help me recognize that everyone is at a different place when it comes to following their path. If there is a change or a shift in my life, show me how to deal with it in a way that honors you. Help me grow for the better because of the deeper understanding you're giving me. I declare that I'm cheering others on instead of sitting in judgment. I declare that my heart leaps as they progress and change, and I'm not going to be a bitter friend or companion. Also help me see and remember that when I'm doing my best through you to understand others, I'm not burdened by what's not my responsibility or by what I can't change. Help me embrace healthy disagreements, as it is a sign I have honest relationships around me. People change, and I'm not the one they need to answer to. They answer to you, God. You are supreme, and today I will no longer make other people's choices about me. Amen.

Chapter 29

Worry or Peace

> Do not be anxious about anything, but in
> everything by prayer and supplication with
> thanksgiving let your requests be made
> known to God. And the peace of God, which
> surpasses all understanding, will guard your
> hearts and your minds in Christ Jesus.
>
> **PHILIPPIANS 4:6-7**

Don't worry about anything, but pray about everything. Right.
Easier said than done.

I don't know about you, but when things get stressful, the last
thing my brain wants to do is calm down and let go. Especially
when I can see something is going wrong or worry a bad moment
is right around the corner. And there are a lot of things to be
stressed and anxious about in the world—from whether we'll fit

in at a party or get the job we want to bigger things like looming pandemics and wars.

Worry is also a natural thing—it was built into us to work as a signal to keep us alert and safe. The problem is, it's way too easy to let that signal become the thing that drives us, the thing that keeps us centered on ourselves and what we think we need to focus on to fix the issue *now*. When we let the panic signal send us to God, however, it frees us to move forward and actually find the safety and comfort we need, and in his timing.

There was one time I thought I'd be late for an event, and I panicked because it looked like there was no way I'd get there safely on time. But in hindsight, God was protecting me and extending time for me. Turns out, the event started late and I arrived right when I needed to, and having an extra two hours of travel gave me time to connect with myself and with God.

When I thought we wouldn't arrive on time, I went into an anxious place, because having enough time and being on time are big things for me. But then I had a conversation with heaven. Heaven revealed to me that all would be well. I just had to trust God was holding it down for me. After all, he's the author of time.

My struggles with time at that point didn't only have to do with how long in the day something took. I also struggled with finances—my bag—worrying I didn't have enough money saved up and thinking I always had to work for more. These money worries got especially strong during 2020 and 2021 because Covid meant I couldn't tour or do events to earn money the way I always had. I know our income is associated with time, and investments take a while to build up and can ebb and flow, but I had to take my own time to learn to trust his Word and let my worries go. Like Deuteronomy 8:17–18 says, "Beware lest you say in your heart, 'My power and the might of my hand have gotten me this wealth.' You shall remember the LORD your God, for it is he who gives you power to get wealth." God will give you the money you need, and he'll make the appointments and get you resources and solutions you need. We just have to go to him in prayer and ask.

And when it comes to time, that's something we need to let go of and give to God as well. Our worrying about something for a moment or for a month won't get it done any faster if it's not meant to happen yet on God's calendar. If something *is* meant to happen, God is in and he's on it. Plus, for God, time doesn't work like it does for me and you—like 2 Peter 3:8 says, "With the Lord one day is as a thousand years, and a thousand years as one day." That's also one reason the Bible tells us to let go of worry and give it to God in prayer. We should stop being anxious and worrying about our days and our future and give it to God and trust him with it. By doing that, we're also building up our faith and trust in God.

Of course, not all worry and panic have to do with future things. We can beat ourselves up with anxiety over things that happened in the past too and let it continue on into our present, so we're stuck in a loop that leads toward self-doubt and added worry. We will struggle and we'll never get past the mental dungeon our feelings have put us in. This is where we really need to lean on God in prayer and let the Spirit speak. When our brain tells us we're worthless because of something that happened, the Spirit can remind us of our real worth as God's child, as well as open our eyes to the people who value us for who we are and can build us up. When we think a past experience means things will never get better in that area, the Spirit reminds us that God controls time and he knows what will happen, which means what we went through had a reason and we can press forward—knowing the past doesn't always predict the present and future.

All that said, I know tapping into that Spirit knowledge is hard when your mind is spinning. Here are some verses you can read and pray when you feel worry and anxiety creeping in, which can help you center your mind and remember God has you:

FEAR

- Deuteronomy 31:8 (NIV): "The LORD himself goes before you and will be with you; he will never leave you nor forsake you. Do not be afraid; do not be discouraged."
- Isaiah 43:1: "Fear not, for I have redeemed you; I have called you by name, you are mine."
- Isaiah 41:10: "Fear not, for I am with you; be not dismayed, for I am your God. I will strengthen you, I will help you, I will uphold you with my righteous right hand."

ANXIETY

- Matthew 6:25–26: "Therefore I tell you, do not be anxious about your life, what you will eat or what you will drink, nor about your body, what you will put on. Is not life more than food, and the body more than clothing? Look at the birds of the air: they neither sow nor reap nor gather into barns, and yet your heavenly Father feeds them. Are you not of more value than they?"
- Jeremiah 29:11: "For I know the plans I have for you, declares the LORD, plans for welfare and not for evil, to give you a future and a hope."

- John 14:27 (NIV): "Peace I leave with you; my peace I give you. I do not give to you as the world gives. Do not let your hearts be troubled and do not be afraid."

PEACE

- Philippians 4:7 (NLT): "Then you will experience God's peace, which exceeds anything we can understand. His peace will guard your hearts and minds as you live in Christ Jesus."
- John 16:33: "I have said these things to you, that in me you may have peace. In the world you will have tribulation. But take heart; I have overcome the world."
- Matthew 11:28–30 (NLT): "Come to me, all of you who are weary and carry heavy burdens, and I will give you rest. Take my yoke upon you. Let me teach you, because I am humble and gentle at heart, and you will find rest for your souls. For my yoke is easy to bear, and the burden I give you is light."

Prayer

Philippians 4:6–7 reminds me, "Do not be anxious about anything, but in every situation, by prayer and petition, with thanksgiving, present your requests to God. And the peace of God, which transcends all understanding, will guard your hearts and your minds in Christ Jesus" (NIV). May the peace that you've left with me guard my heart and overtake any anxious thought. May it overthrow any worry. Thank you for guarding my heart and mind as your Word promises. I enjoy talking to you. You soothe and calm me when you're present. I promise to surrender to you. No worry will overtake me, because I know I can better handle it with you by my side. You will send the help I truly need if I only ask. My trust in you is growing every day, and you are more powerful than anything this world can throw at me. Thank you! Amen.

Self-Sabotage

> *Cast your burden on the* LORD, *and*
> *he will sustain you; he will never*
> *permit the righteous to be moved.*
>
> **PSALM 55:22**

Okay, so my question is . . . how do you deal with self-sabotage? Does self-sabotaging come from the enemy or is it a mind game? And does overthinking play into self-sabotage?

I think the source is a combination of us overthinking and the way the enemy uses that overthinking to drag us further into doubts about ourselves and what we experience.

We can make a moment bigger than it is, and then take ourselves into a sink hole with just our imagination—causing depression or anxiety that feeds the cycle. Now that I understand that what I think can affect who I am, and that the Spirit is always alongside me to help, I am very aggressive with myself in prayer and conversations. Being patient with yourself also plays a role.

As a result, I try to talk things through with someone to ensure I'm not overthinking. Usually my family or friends have been able to push me back into a happy/reasonable place—redirecting me from my negative thoughts or anxious feelings.

The enemy can guilt-trip us into this place too. As he is the "accuser of the brethren," it's his job to get you to consider his suggestions, or to make us feel bad about things we do or choices we make, to the point we feel we are too far gone and can't change.

However, a way to defeat this is to know Scripture and remember we're more powerful than him. Even in the darkest of moments, there is going to be a voice—the Spirit—reminding you of the truth of who you are. I don't have to accept anything the devil tries to send my way. I can test the lies against the truth. That's my way of fighting that battle. I start speaking things aloud as well, when my mind is going haywire. I also write declarations I can speak when certain struggles arise, which has helped me tap into the Spirit's guidance.

When you feel yourself slipping into self-sabotage and doubt, take a moment to stop and assess what is true. Because if you take that moment to breathe and evaluate, the truth can bubble up and start attacking the lies. Remember who you are inside, and the fact you have a heavenly Father who literally lives inside you to help you fight these battles in your brain. Say affirmations out loud if it helps, or write them down and stick them on your mirror or computer or wherever you need the reminders.

And if depression or anxiety show up several times a week or month, go find a professional—seriously, don't wait a moment—because what you see as "self-sabotage" can be something bigger and is nothing to mess with. It's also not something you should ever have to deal with alone. (And if your inner voice is telling you that you aren't worth it, that's a lie from the enemy you need to kick out immediately.) Even if it seems like the emotions and thoughts are all-consuming to the point they've swallowed everything else, there are people who will support you through the pain and self-doubts, working with you to find a path forward. A brighter future. Finding a professional you feel comfortable talking with can make a huge difference.

God made us to conquer and gave us the Holy Spirit to arm us against the attack. There are going to be times we feel tired and worn during the battle, but that doesn't mean we can't triumph in the end. Knock down that self-sabotage and stand strong in the knowledge you have a powerful God and an inner Guide always with you to help you fight and persevere, one who can lead you to people and tools that help you win.

Chapter 30

The Mystery and the Truth

> *For we were all baptized by one Spirit*
> *so as to form one body and we were*
> *all given the one Spirit to drink.*
>
> **1 CORINTHIANS 12:13** NIV

As we've been exploring the Holy Spirit, there may have been some stories that sounded very different from anything you've ever experienced or grew up with, or you might have been nodding right along because you've also felt the power of the Spirit come over you or heard a distinct voice telling you something you sensed was from God. That's because while there's only one Holy Spirit, the ways we as human beings *understand* him can sometimes be quite different from person to person.

Part of the reason is that because we're human, the Holy Spirit is always going to be mysterious to us. While there's a lot we've looked at in this book, based on what we can know from the Bible and what God shows us, there is a lot more about the Spirit we simply can't understand or grasp because we live in a physical world, not the fully spiritual one he operates in. Our brains just can't get themselves around it. (For example, try thinking about the fact there is one God, but God is also three beings—Father, Son, and Holy Spirit—who exist separately at the same time. The Trinity is a basic part of Christianity we all accept, but even theologians don't completely understand everything about it!)

And while do know from Scripture that the Spirit is guiding us, reminding us of God's love and plan for us, helping us navigate life, and gifting us to serve God, the mystery factor means exactly *how* the Spirit does those things can be interpreted differently by some church traditions. For example, some churches have very different views on the way the Spirit intercedes in our lives and how exactly he makes himself known in our world.

The biggest difference in how churches see the Spirit probably has to do with how they understand the Spirit's gifts—how he gives them, when he gives them, and exactly what they are. For churches that believe in baptism in the Spirit—which is similar to Pentecost in the Bible, where believers receive the Spirit in a powerful way and unlock their spiritual gifts—the Spirit comes to spiritually baptized people in the gift of tongues, feeling the presence inside them, in visions, or other powerful ways. They point to the disciples and apostles having the gifts of tongues and having the Spirit physically come to them and speak to them as proof of how the Spirit can work today. I come from this kind of tradition, and I've seen the Spirit make himself known through someone's heightened gift to intuit spiritual messages, like my aunt, and have felt the Spirit come on me many times. But there are also churches that see baptism in the Spirit in a different way—that it happens when you accept Jesus as your Savior, and that the Spirit is able to use and enhance the gifts God has given you like the ability to lead, or nurture, or minister and share the gospel with others. In these traditions, things like spiritual encounters or visions aren't talked about as much, and if they are, they're usually discussed more along the lines of special events that happen in some people's lives.

Sometimes we can get hung up on these differences as followers of Christ, but the fact is, there is a lot more we can all agree on as Christians that is much more important to us as believers—namely, that God is working in our lives and wants to have a relationship with us, and he's using the Spirit to do it. When Jesus left Earth and went up to heaven, that meant God's earthly presence in the form of a human was leaving us too, and that's why Jesus sent us the Spirit—a part of God, who also lived in Jesus and helped guide him throughout his ministry. The Spirit is what allowed Christians in the Bible to do everything they did during their ministries, and it has also allowed everyone who's followed Jesus to this day to do amazing things for God. Exactly what that spiritual gift is and exactly how we interpret it doesn't matter so much. What does matter is that we listen to the nudges and intuitions and dreams and everything else God's Spirit sends us and use the gifts he gives us so we can all be God's hands and feet in the world, however he makes that happen.

That also means that if there are some things you still are working to understand when it comes to the Spirit, that's okay! And honestly, we're all there to some degree. Just pray, talk to people who you trust to guide you, and read your Bible while asking for guidance and direction. God is there for you. The Spirit is in you. Trust the vibes you feel.

Prayer

Father, I may not always understand how the Spirit is working in my life, but I know it's there and it's from you. Help me learn to know your voice and listen when I hear it. Get me on your vibrations so I can feel when you are calling me, and so I can sense when you are close. Don't let me get so hung up on the details that I miss the big picture of what you're doing in my life. I also know you've been guiding me all along, and I thank you for your love and care for me. I want to show others your awesome power and the amazing things that happen when your children walk with you. Make me attuned to you more and more so I can use my gifts and honor you above all. Amen!

Reflection Questions

Introduction

1. What has been your experience with the Holy Spirit?
2. What are you wanting to learn, gain, and/or understand about the Holy Spirit as you read this book?
3. Read Psalm 143:10. Write out a simple prayer in your own words similar to this verse, capturing what you want God to show you.

Chapter 1–The Unction: "Somethin' Told Me"

1. Think back on a time in your life when you know the Holy Spirit was working in that situation.
2. How did you respond? Was it with joy, fear, confusion, or something else?
3. How do you see God working in your present circumstances?
4. Based on John 14:26, write a prayer of thanksgiving for the Holy Spirit.

Chapter 2–I Ran for My Life

1. How do you understand your spiritual gift(s)?
2. In what ways have you attempted to understand your gift(s)? Are there any gifts you feel you may have overlooked or discounted before?
3. In what ways have you used your gift(s)? Are there any new ways you might be able to use them now?
4. Here are some Scriptures that list spiritual gifts: 1 Corinthians 12, Romans 12, and Ephesians 4. As you read through these passages, craft a prayer about your desire concerning spiritual gifts.

Chapter 3–Get Out!

1. Think back on a situation in which you were stuck (maybe "stuck on stupid"). How did the Holy Spirit speak to you? Or how is he speaking to you now?
2. In Psalm 40, David expressed a prayer of thanksgiving to God for lifting him out of a difficult situation. Write out or say a similar prayer thanking God for what he's done in your life, or a prayer expressing the desire of your heart concerning your present situation.

Chapter 4–Eagles in the Sky

1. Think back on a time when the Holy Spirit used nature to speak to you.
2. What was the message God was attempting to convey then? What is he trying to tell you now?
3. As you read Ephesians 1:17–18 (read the entire chapter if you have time), write out or express a prayer to the Lord asking for opened eyes so you notice the signs he sends.

Chapter 5—Playing Church

1. How would you describe the difference between the times you were just playing church and the times you truly believed you were connecting with the Holy Spirit?

2. In John 16:13, the Holy Spirit identifies himself as our guide. In what ways has he guided you in the past and presently?

3. Voice or write out a prayer in an area where you need his guidance. Don't be afraid to try a fleece prayer—just be willing to watch for the signs!

Chapter 6—Mind-Body-Vibe

1. Do you believe your life right now is balanced or unbalanced? Write out some examples.

2. How would you describe your times of rest and self-care? Ask the Holy Spirit to reveal what needs to increase or decrease in this area.

3. Write out Bible verses, word pictures, wise advice previously given to you, or any thoughts God brings to mind. Pray over what has been revealed to you. Surrender to the Father so he can do his job of making changes in your heart.

Chapter 7—Knocked Off Your Square

1. In what ways has Satan has knocked you off your square?

2. What can you do to get back in order and/or prevent the enemy from keeping you in a state of confusion?

3. Various places in the Bible portray the enemy (Satan) as a hungry lion looking for prey. How does this picture scare you? How does it empower you?

4. What is a prayer you can pray when he attacks, which reflects who you are in Christ? (If you need some inspiration about what to ask for, look up Ephesians 6:10–12.)

Chapter 8–Checkmate or Check Yourself

1. Think about a time God had to check you, guide you back into line. How was that experience? How has it helped you navigate similar situations now?
2. Ask the Holy Spirit for his loving examination. Make his revelations a prayer of praise, thanksgiving, confession, and commitment.

Chapter 9–Conversations Vs. Prayers

1. Ask the Holy Spirit to bring to mind any situation or person you may be holding a grudge against. Now write out a prayer expressing what you desire for God to do in your heart concerning the person(s) involved in the offense.
2. It's okay to express grief, anger, frustration, or any other emotion after you've been hurt. If you need someone to walk with you through this process, ask God to bring someone to mind and make the call—today.

Chapter 10–The Heart Matters

1. Ask God to bring to mind a past hurt you may not have even realized still affects you. Confess honestly to the Father about what hurt you about the situation and any ill feelings you still hold on to because of the offense. (If the situation is similar to the one you prayed about in chapter 9, continue to work through that issue.)

2. Look up Bible verses that deal with what you're facing right now in your heart—be it doubt, mistrust, a need to feel in control, or anxiety that makes it hard to let go and move forward. If you get stuck, go online and search for "Bible verses that talk about [issue]," or reach out to a pastor or trusted advisor in the faith who could help.

3. Take a moment to ask the Holy Spirit to speak to you in the coming days. What thoughts and ideas come to mind as you pay attention to what God sends? Are there any recurring ideas or behaviors you have new clarity on?

Chapter 11—Keep Dreaming

1. Think back on a dream you may have had that made you stop and think. Could it be from God? What makes you think that?

2. In what ways did the Holy Spirit confirm the dream? Did it come true? Did God give you a Scripture passage or a conversation about the dream with a wiser, mature Christian?

3. Ask the Holy Spirit in a prayer to make his voice clear to you, especially as you study the Bible while considering the dream.

Chapter 12—Baggage

1. In Psalm 139:24, King David asked God to search him, to make sure nothing offensive lurked inside. Take some time to ask God to search you. Write down what the Holy Spirit brings to mind.

2. Share with a Christian friend what the Lord is showing you and ask if they would pray with you and for you concerning these issues.

3. Now think about any bags you may be carrying—how can you work to unpack them, starting today? What bags can you leave behind completely?

Chapter 13–Who's All Over There?

1. Recall a time you experienced the weight of the "elephant in the room." How did you respond or react in that situation?
2. Now, in hindsight, what could you have done or said differently?
3. Write out a brief prayer and ask for the Holy Spirit's help to know how you can be a child of light in all situations.

Chapter 14–Solo Dolo

1. Think about the last time you were in isolation—either planned or forced. What kind of thoughts/prayers/self-conversations did you fill your time with?
2. Write out an invitation to the Holy Spirit and describe the next time you are alone together. Will you discuss things or stay quiet? Will you engage in a project (art, music, writing) or just be still?

Chapter 15–Who's Who?

1. Think about your relationships. Are you pleased or displeased?
2. What areas of your relationships need to change?
3. Who else needs to be included in the circle of people you have around you?
4. Ask the Holy Spirit's help to reach out and help you discern relationships. Are there some that need to be

strengthened and others that need to be let go? Pray about your decision.

Chapter 16—Sound Check

1. Think about the people in your life who have helped you grow by being honest and upfront with you. Write down their names.
2. How can you enlarge the number of people giving wise counsel to you?
3. Take the time to thank God for those who care enough to confront you when needed.

Chapter 17—Perfect Harmony

1. Think back on an experience that was difficult but you "left too soon," or "stayed too long." How was the Holy Spirit involved or not involved in that experience?
2. Say or write out a prayer of thanksgiving for what you went through and what you learned. Add a request for the Holy Spirit's guidance in what you are involved in now or in the future.

Chapter 18—Say It with Honey

1. How do people respond to your communication style? Do they take a step back because you are abrasive? Love to talk to you because you are a listener, friendly, and kind? Can't understand you, so you're often asked to repeat or explain what you mean?
2. What changes do you need to make in the way you talk to people?
3. Pray about making that transformation within yourself.

Chapter 19—Girls' Night Out

1. Think about the last time you and a group of friends got together and had a really good time. What made it special? The event? The people? The conversation?
2. Thank the Holy Spirit for pulling that all together for you. Recognize his presence and his plan.
3. If you don't currently have a close group of friends, ask God to guide you, and also to give you the confidence to step out and take a chance on building a relationship.

Chapter 20—I Hear Voices

1. Put yourself in the place of Samuel, who desired to hear from the Lord. How would you have reacted?
2. Think about the time you need to set aside, the place, and your attitude, if you want to hear from God. How can you make those moments happen?
3. Pray about adjustments that need to be made so you can become more acquainted and familiar with the voice of the Holy Spirit.

Chapter 21—The Vibe of Your Music: What Is It Making You Do?

1. What song or songs often repeat in your mind? How is the music uplifting you?
2. What needs to change, and how is the Holy Spirit directing you to make changes?
3. Pray specifically for things you may need to do differently in this area—including asking for the power to avoid songs that negatively affect you.

Chapter 22–Spiritual Junk Food

1. What areas of your life might be junk food—things you enjoy but that are getting in the way of living a healthier life? What can you do to start cutting back your cravings?

2. Now think of things that make you feel whole and full—that make you feel like a better version of yourself. What can you do to pursue those things more closely? Is there a friend or mentor who can help you?

3. Think about starting a journal to record your experiences as you try to shift away from the junk. Are there any big changes you notice as you page back over time?

Chapter 23–No Discounts

1. Are there times you feel you need to hold yourself back or not do something in order to fit in? How does that feel? What would it be like to follow the voice in your gut?

2. Take a piece of paper and write down the things you feel you are gifted in. Now ask a friend or trusted person to add to the list, and think about what they see in you. Does looking at the entire list make you feel different about your value and what you feel called to be in the world?

Chapter 24–Proximity Vibe

1. Think about your proximity vibe aroma—how would you describe it? Is it a sweet smell, or is something off? Who do you think might be contributing to that scent?

2. Now think about "smells" in your life you may have
   become used to over time. Write them down here—or if
   you prefer, in a place you can keep private. How can the
   Spirit help you become more aware of those odors, and
   help you get rid of them for good?

3. Now ask God to come into your life and help peel back
   the layers. Over the next few weeks and months, make
   notes of times you can feel those old layers coming off
   and a new, fresher scent coming off you instead. Also
   note how the change makes you feel!

Chapter 25–I Washed a Stranger's Feet

1. When you hear the word humility, what comes to mind?
   It is a positive word or a negative one to you? Why do
   you think you feel that way?

2. Think about areas in your life where you could show
   more humility. If you feel stuck at all, focus on one part
   of your life—school, home, work. What one thing could
   you do for someone to show you're symbolically washing
   their feet?

3. Ask God to help you tap into that humble part of Jesus
   inside you, and then make mental notes when you see
   your servant mindset making a kingdom difference for
   someone else.

Chapter 26–The Dating Pool

1. Have you ever made a list of the "perfect boyfriend"?
   What kinds of things are/would be on that list now? Has
   that list changed at all after reading this chapter?

2. Take a moment to ask God to help you in your romantic

relationships—be that during a time of singleness or in a dating relationship you're in now. What signs and nudges do you feel? Are there any vibes (good or bad) you noticed before but dismissed that come to a new light now?

3. How can you work on your emotional intelligence? Think about reaching out to a trusted friend or advisor to help you grow in this area.

Chapter 27—All Over the Place

1. Is there any clutter in your life you want to get rid of? Just like when we're cleaning a giant mess, sometimes it can be overwhelming if we try to fix it all at once. Take a moment to ask the Spirit to help you see the steps you need to take to get started, and then pray for the strength to start a new habit of keeping things clearer in the future.

2. When you next attend a church service or Bible study, take a moment to listen for any signs that are being set up on your spiritual street. Is there anything the Spirit is trying to help you move toward?

Chapter 28—People Change

1. Is there anyone in your life who seems to be struggling right now, or who you need to extend grace to after a tough moment together? If you are close to them, schedule a time to connect, and listen to what they want to share. If it's someone you aren't that close with, but you feel a pull to do something, pray or take time to give them a kind word of support.

2. Think about who you were when you started reading this book, and who you are now. What changes have you seen in your thinking? How have those changes shifted how you see the people around you? Now think of ways you can use your new knowledge to strengthen your relationships and grow even more.

3. If you feel led, grab a notebook and start keeping a daily journal, so you can see how God is working in you—and working in the people around you. Keep a special eye out for patterns or shifts that can help you see where God is leading you, and *who* he may be leading you to in friendships and mentor relationships.

Chapter 29—Worry or Peace

1. When something is causing you anxiety or worry, try writing it on a piece of paper. Then talk to God about that worry—how it's made you feel, and how you'd like him to help you with it. Afterward, put the piece of paper in a box and keep it near a place you like to pray or relax. Occasionally open the box, look at the slips of paper, and pray over any that still nag at you. Have you noticed any changes in the level of worry or things that have happened around it each time you check and pray?

2. Is there a constant worry from something in your past, or a current worry that won't go away? Especially if this worry is affecting your mental health, talk to someone today—like a trusted friend, a counselor, or a mentor. You don't have to deal with it on your own, and there is strength in getting help! God wants us to have a life of freedom and health.

Chapter 30–The Mystery and the Truth

1. As you've read this book, do you feel like you have a better understanding of who the Holy Spirit is and how he works? In what ways have you sensed the Spirit working in your life?

2. Are there any big questions you still have? If so, that's natural! Write them down here and reach out to your pastor or a trusted mentor to talk them through. Also ask them for any resources, books, or Bible passages they recommend that could help you explore the Spirit more and grow your understanding.